Cybersecurity Leadership for Healthcare Organizations and Institutions of Higher Education

RIVER PUBLISHERS SERIES IN DIGITAL SECURITY AND FORENSICS

The "River Publishers Series in Security and Digital Forensics" is a series of comprehensive academic and professional books which focus on the theory and applications of Cyber Security, including Data Security, Mobile and Network Security, Cryptography and Digital Forensics. Topics in Prevention and Threat Management are also included in the scope of the book series, as are general business Standards in this domain.

Books published in the series include research monographs, edited volumes, handbooks and textbooks. The books provide professionals, researchers, educators, and advanced students in the field with an invaluable insight into the latest research and developments.

Topics covered in the series include:-

- Blockchain for secure transactions
- Cryptography
- Cyber Security
- Data and App Security
- Digital Forensics
- Hardware Security
- IoT Security
- Mobile Security
- Network Security
- Privacy
- Software Security
- Standardization
- Threat Management

For a list of other books in this series, visit www.riverpublishers.com

Cybersecurity Leadership for Healthcare Organizations and Institutions of Higher Education

Bradley Fowler
Member of National Cyber Watch Association, USA

Bruce G. Chaundy
Southern New Hampshire University, USA

River Publishers

Routledge
Taylor & Francis Group
NEW YORK AND LONDON

Published 2025 by River Publishers
River Publishers
Alsbjergvej 10, 9260 Gistrup, Denmark
www.riverpublishers.com

Distributed exclusively by Routledge
605 Third Avenue, New York, NY 10017, USA
4 Park Square, Milton Park, Abingdon, Oxon OX14 4RN

Cybersecurity Leadership for Healthcare Organizations and Institutions of Higher Education / Bradley Fowler and Bruce G. Chaundy.

Routledge is an imprint of the Taylor & Francis Group, an informa business

ISBN 978-87-7004-234-5 (hardback)
ISBN 978-87-7004-784-5 (paperback)
ISBN 978-87-7004-777-7 (online)
ISBN 978-8-770-04776-0 (ebook master)

Contents

Acknowledgments

Education has been the key to propel my ability to become the researcher and writer I have become. Thus, it is imperative I render acknowledgment to each institution of higher education I have been honored to attend and gain invaluable knowledge from. Those institutions include Penn Foster College, Ashford University, Florida Institute of Technology, Capella University, University of Arizona Global Campus, Bellevue University, American Public University Systems, University of Maryland Global Campus, Wilmington University, California Coast University, University of Phoenix, and Capitol Technology University.

Dr. Ian McAndrew, your commitment to empower students at every level of their educational journey is phenomenal and greatly appreciated! Thank you!

Douglas Rausch, CISSP, your commitment to inspire cybersecurity and information assurance, students to be their best is greatly appreciated. Thank you for the countless number of supporting recommendation letters you have provided me over the last 6 years.

Dr. Patricia Insley and Dr. Cindy Brownell, it was your tenacious persistence that propelled me to become the writer I am today. There were times I felt like walking away from my Doctor of Education, but your patience and support helped me overcome that obstacle. Thank you!

A special thank you is extended to my editors and production team. Love and admiration are rendered to my mother for continuing to believe in me, Jay and Jason, thank you both. Kitturah and Amaya, love you. Will, Alex, Xavier, Blake, and Bryce, cousins, family-in-law, and long-lost associates, ex-bed partners, and ex-lovers; thank you for your support and envy over the last ten years, that became the source of my motivation to keep going.

God, Thank You!

List of Figures

List of Tables

List of Abbreviations

API	Application programming interface
AWS	Amazon Web Services
BIOS	Basic input/output system
CanSSOC	Canadian Shared Security Operations Centre
CERT	Computer Emergency Response Team
CIA	Confidentiality, integrity, and availability
CIO	Chief information officer
CIPT	Continuous internal penetration testing
CISA	Cybersecurity Information Sharing Act
CISM	Certified information security manager
CISSP	Certified information systems security professional
CNSS	Committee on National Security Systems
CVE	Common exposures and vulnerabilities
DDOS	Distributed denial of service
DDOSA	Distributed denial of service attack
EDI	Electronic data interchange
EHR	Elastic health record
ENISA	European Network and Information Security Agency
FISMA	Federal Information Security Modernization Act
FOIA	Freedom of Information Act
GAI	General artificial intelligence
GDPR	General Data Protection Regulation
GLBA	Gramm–Leach–Bliley Act
GUI	Graphical user interface
HIPAA	Health Insurance Probability and Accountability Act
HITRUST	Health Information Trust Alliance
HTTPS	Hypertext transport protocol security
I/O	Industrial organizational
IaaS	Infrastructure as a Service
ICT	Information communication technology
IDS	Intrusion detection systems
ISP	Internet service provider

ISTC	Information systems, information technology, and cloud
LAN	Local access network
MDR	Managed detection and response
NLP	Natural language processing
NSA	National Security Agency
OS	Operating system
OWASP	Open Web Application Security Project
PCI-DSS	Payment Card Industry-Data Security Standard
PCRE	Perl Compatible Regular Expressions
PPD	Presidential Policy Directive
RAID	Redundant Array of Independent Disks
RDP	Remote desktop protocol
SaaS	Software as a Service
SDLC	System development life cycle
SFTP	Secure file transfer protocol
SHRM	Society of Human Resource Managers
SIEM	Security information event management
SLA	Service level agreement
UNGA	United Nations General Assembly
VPN	Virtual private network
WAN	Wide access network
Wi-Fi	Wireless Fidelity
WPA/WPA2	Wi-Fi Protected Access

Introduction

Two of the world's leading innovative industries are facing tremendous hurdles defending their information systems and information technology networks and information assets from cyberattack. Despite continued efforts to improve strategies and methodologies of deterrence and prevention, healthcare organizations and institutions of higher education have become prime targets for cybercriminals because of the value invested in the information assets these two industry leaders collect, store, transmit, and share. The information value is embedded in consumer's names, addresses, phone numbers, email accounts, bank account details, health record information, date of birth, and social security numbers and places these entities at the top of cybercriminals' lists of attention. Then when you consider the value of health and medical research developed by healthcare organizations, the patents they register, and intellectual property these entities own, the value of this information increases. Institutions of higher education embody information relating to student's records, including their names, degree of study, parents' social security numbers, student's social security numbers, home addresses, bank routing numbers for direct deposit of staff and faculty, and research data stored in institutional databases. Together, both healthcare organizations and institutions of higher education accumulate well over $10 million in information assets annually.

Research compiled from computer security researchers in China, Germany, Japan, the United Kingdom, and the United States reported in 2019 that cyberattacks involving Internet of Things (IoT) were increasing due to the lack of effective security configuration of medical devices utilized for healthcare organizations patient care. This attack on IoT devices established an attack method that remains untamed and incapable of reduction in 2024. Furthermore, research conveyed that 10 million or more medical devices are connected to patient's medical beds globally, increasing potential risk of these type of cyberattacks. Research also reports that manufacturers of medical devices are aware of the security risk concerns, admitting these devices are not effectively secured when operating in healthcare organizations. This impacts the ability for cybersecurity to be effective, despite the continued efforts to modify the security risks enveloped in these technology-integrated devices. Thus, healthcare organizations worldwide are now forced to build stronger alliances and begin exchanging information about these individual cyberattack incidents, to help prepare other healthcare organizations, which have not experienced the same attack methods. It is believed doing so can be instrumental in helping these entities improve their own strategies to deter successful cyberattacks. However, limited research stagnates these efforts globally.

Research also reports that higher education institutions in the United Kingdom continue experiencing a rise in cyberattacks, with no end in sight. These attacks are causing institutions of higher education in the UK to increase awareness training for faculty and staff, increase hiring of IT professionals, and increase cybersecurity leadership. One concern these institutions have is a limited share of knowledge regarding the various types of cyberattack methods being deployed. This stagnates the ability for these institutions to gain leverage over cyberattackers and decrease the threat of cyberattack victimization. Research also reports that UK universities are being targeted because of their research facilities. The embedded value in scholarly research invokes cybercriminals to risk being caught by officials. And because these institutions remain tied to outdated software application systems, ineffective information technology configurations, and a lack of trained and cyber defense-ready IT practitioners; institutions of higher education in the United Kingdom face an uphill battle to control risk and decrease vulnerabilities integrated in their information systems and information technology.

These risks are not particularly known risks. While some institutions of higher education utilize Windows operating systems 7–11, some institutions are relying on Unix/Linux OS. This can be complex for IT practitioners to govern effectively when they are limited in their knowledge of these systems and the required security configuration settings needed to secure these applications. Then when you consider the scale of risk woven in all software applications relied on for daily business communication and transactions, the complexity of managing these systems with limited impact of risk, becomes narrow.

Thus, IT practitioners in healthcare organizations and institutions of higher education need to partner with IT/cybersecurity leaders, who embody the research expertise and knowledge that helps provide validated and verifiable information to increase security awareness and reduce the ability of cybercrime incident victimization. Although there are IT/cybersecurity leaders around the world, who are doing their best to provide significant research and information that supports IT/cybersecurity leaders. There is a growing need for additional research experts who possess the training, education, experience, and knowledge about cybersecurity, cybersecurity policy, managing information systems, cloud computing architecture, information assurance, and technology management.

Dr. Bradley Fowler has spent the last 16 years investing in studying these subjects at top- tier national academic centers of excellence designated by the U.S. Department of Homeland Security and the National Security Agency. Mr. Fowler thrives to share his knowledge through his previously published scholarly textbooks on cybersecurity public policy, AWS cloud computing architecture, information assurance risk management strategies, cyberpsychology, and cybersecurity leadership. However, this textbook delivers a new approach to managing and understanding cybersecurity leadership for healthcare organizations and institutions of higher education through the integration of artificial intelligence, machine learning, natural language processing, and industrial organizational psychology.

Utilization of artificial intelligence (AI), machine learning (ML), and natural language processing (NLP) as key methods to manage cyberattacks and reduce cyber risk and vulnerabilities, through algorithms and data analytics, provides organized and structured information regarding similarities, indifferences, and patterns of activities previously deployed in cyberattacks targeting healthcare organizations and institutions of higher education. This research can help you improve your knowledge of AI, ML, and NLP as effective tools in supporting the research needed to improve organizational structure of cyberattacks and cybersecurity leadership. Possessing this knowledge can reduce concerns of risk associated with software commonly utilized in healthcare organizations and institutions of higher education because this tool of learning is a reference you can rely on. Inside are lists of artificial intelligence tools, you can begin understanding to help resolve some of your concerns of how to effectively manage risk associated with networks, Wi-Fi, and usage of the Internet and intranet.

In addition, you gain access to a lists of digital forensics tools, including Snort, Nmap, Zenmap, and Wireshark, and applications utilized for Windows, Unix/Linux, and Mac operating systems. Having this knowledge provides leverage over your adversaries and prepares you to implement new infrastructures that compete with competitors and out leverage cybercriminals. Possessing this knowledge enables you to implement effective methods of assessing, developing, implementing, and managing cybersecurity leadership and policy. Lacking the ability to effectively develop policies to control risks enveloped in the workplace impacts your ability to control risk internally and externally.

Thus, this learning reference shares details in understanding National Institute of Standards and Technology recommended guidelines. These policies have become instrumental in supporting the improvement of workplace cybersecurity training for IT practitioners and deployment of auditing, assessment of information systems and technology, and cloud-based environment. Furthermore, this learning reference provides knowledge regarding industrial organizational (I/O) psychology; providing essential information about the role this industry leading concept plays in helping organizations and corporations improve the cognitive thinking skills of personnel that improves the overall cybersecurity defense needed in organizations and corporations. When you complete this research, you will have increased your knowledge of digital forensics through the embedded reference guide, and be 10 steps ahead of cyberattacks, and understand what you are required to do to increase your cybersecurity leadership against cybercriminals targeting healthcare organizations and institutions of higher education. Each chapter envelopes learning objectives to guide your comprehension of the content delivery, closes with a summary and investigative scenario to help you review issues as they relate to real-world security problems. Discussion questions are embedded as well to ensure you reassess your learning experience, and a glossary provides meaning for keywords.

1

Current Trends in Cybersecurity Leadership

Learning Objectives

- Distinguish the meaning of cybersecurity.
- Assess trends in cybersecurity leadership.
- Acknowledge effective cybersecurity leadership planning from 1990s to 2000s.
- Interpret methods of future trends in cybersecurity leadership.

1.1 Introduction

Cybersecurity leadership has grown exponentially since cybersecurity began growing popular in the late 1990s. Since then, the United States Department of Homeland Security, the National Security Agency, the White House, and various branches of the United States federal agencies, i.e., Federal Bureau of Investigations, Central Intelligence Agency, the United States Department of Justice, and local community law enforcement, have begun working in concert with United States Congress, to enact and mandate laws that define how government entities, businesses, nonprofits, and citizens must act and respond to cyber activities deployed across the Internet. This growing push for legislative control and law enforcement encompasses the four cyber domains: land, air, sea, and space. However, despite doing so there remains a need for continued growth of federal legislation to meet the wide scope of cybercrime and cyberattack incidents weaving into the mainstream of business and social society. This criminal behavior consistently impedes communities, domestically and internationally. Thus, to minimize these attacks, methods of deterrence are being applied to thwart the erosion of world economies and the impact this malicious activity has on the lives of global citizens. Therefore, cybersecurity leaders must become aware of the issues and trends enveloping cybercrime and cyberculture, and understand what it takes to gain control over the risk cybercrime and cyberculture has both internally and externally.

Additionally, cybersecurity leaders must deploy activities that will stop cybercriminals from gaining leverage to defeat law enforcement from winning the war on cybercrime. After all, not only is the United States wrestling to enact laws and policy that help manage and control the onset of cybercrime incidents. The European Commission is implementing cybersecurity laws and policy. One significant law imposed is the General Data Protection Regulation (GDPR). This law was enacted to enforce a standard of protecting consumer's personal identifiable information. Additional laws are being assessed and adopted internationally as a method of deterrence. But with the enactment of new cyber laws and policy, there are also concerns enveloping human rights as they align with the individual's usage of the Internet. Therefore, there remains a need to understand what cybersecurity leadership is and how this authoritative leadership role must be managed and integrated in public and private sector.

This chapter provides some history about cybersecurity leadership, domestically and internationally. First, you will learn about cyberattack methods and incidents that began in the 1990s, and quickly shift into the 2000s, to assess what strategies were implemented to upgrade methods of managing cybercrime through cybersecurity leadership. You will also gain insight of cybersecurity leadership as it was depicted in 2023 and examine forecasted future trends beyond 2024, to prepare you and your organization, for what awaits us all in coming years according to experts. A summary reiterates what you learn in this chapter; while an investigative scenario helps you distinguish how to define cybersecurity leadership for your organization. In closing, you will complete discussion questions to enable you to reiterate your reading comprehension of this chapter's content.

1.2 1990s

In the 1990s, cybersecurity was born through the efforts of multiple information technology and information systems organizations, countries, and Congressional efforts. Research conveys that discussion of cybersecurity began saturating global agendas during the post-Cold War in the late 1990s. [1] However, it was during the 1980s when computer-related security concerns rose and attracted public attention because of the first cyber virus deployed, i.e., the Brain virus. This virus was deployed by two programmers from Pakistan, who discovered a method of replacing executable code hidden in the boot sector of an old floppy disk. [2] Additional research conveys that the execution of the Morris worm, which surfaced in 1988, and affected Unix noun systems, created the purpose for the Computer Emergency Response

Team (CERT) at Carnegie Mellon University. CERT's primary purpose was to help prevent cyberattacks and establish a framework of response. This organizational approach invoked European countries to increase awareness of cybersecurity. Then in 1995, the first European organization was introduced in Slovakia. The European Network and Information Security Agency (ENISA) embodied all EU member states, and created key international standards for information security as well as established the Slovak legal framework to protect information and additional documents adopted by the Slovak government. [3] This helped establish the need for additional organizations in other countries, including Poland, which resulted from young hackers invading information systems, externally of Poland national border.

Since cyber is considered a realm of space, many assume that any human activity and communication deployed across the Internet should be considered incapable of being controlled by organizations, international laws, and geographical jurisdictions. After all, cyberspace cannot be limited to acts of crime deployed on land via the Internet. Therefore, continued debates rise regarding if usage of cybercrime laws are going to be instrumental in supporting countries and government's ability to thwart cybercriminals' behavior. Thus, despite the growth of information security organizations, universal talk about enacting legal control continued facing tremendous backlash because of the impact this topic has in correlation with human rights.

In fact, when examining research dating back to 1958, one year after Russia launched Sputnik, reports convey that the UN General Assembly developed and introduced a committee responsible for determining what is considered peaceful usage of outer space. [4] Then in 1963, research reports that the UN introduced the Declaration of Legal Principles, which was considered to be responsible for governing the activities of States in the Exploration and usage of outer space. Since then, space laws have been defined through international agreements such as the Outer Space Treaty that was signed in 1967. However, cyberspace is not governed by physical awareness; therefore, nations were believed to not have control to impose restrictions to protect or even threaten activities deployed in a neighboring border patrol. Thus, innovative concepts were required to help define a level of power to utilize influence over cyber domains, as well as define the behaviors classified as noncriminal. One area of debate that continued impacting change of laws and policy in cyber domains involved the military, which is believed to be keen toward emphasizing its own unique method of attracting funding to enable it to explore opportunities. Both the UK Ministry of Defense's Development and the US Department of Defense introduced similar descriptions regarding interdependence on a wide scope of constituent elements, including networks, computer systems, and embedded software. However, it was Dr. John B. Sheldon who defined cyberspace as a four-layer vertical.

Dr. Sheldon believed that the four-layer vertical encompasses the infrastructure layer, which he classifies as the physical layers, i.e., computer hardware, servers, network components, cabling, and satellites. These components are tools of communication and engagement that enable end users to access the Internet through PCs and personal technology devices, i.e., mobile phones, desktop computers, and tablets. Dr. Sheldon adds that the physical layer is second and includes the transmission of data files and assets via the Internet in the infrastructure layer. It is through this layer that fiber optics becomes wireless propagation that connects to Bluetooth and international satellite links. The third layer, i.e., syntactic, encompasses communication protocols, software applications, and network routing algorithms. And the fourth layer embodies the semantic layer, which Dr. Sheldon explains includes the ability for humans to grasp reality through web interfaces and software applications that speak languages understood across borders. This influences the gross domestic product of online business, the rate of web page interface developed, shared, and stored, and the percentage of populations who invest in social media network usage, trends of cybercrimes, and the effectiveness of legislation and law enforcement. These are some of the challenges and issues governments have had to understand and learn how to manage to enact and impose laws and policy regarding cyber domains and the realm of cybercrime governed by cybersecurity leadership.

Another interesting point that empowers the movement toward cybersecurity leadership, domestically, derives from seemingly endless growth of computer attacks that targeted government systems to retrieve sensitive information. These attacks are called distributed denial of service attacks. DDOS attacks are commonly used to prevent citizens from accessing government information websites. This attack mode ushered in increased awareness and effort to make cybersecurity a precedence to control cybercriminal activity through cybersecurity leadership. Additional attack methods that made headlines included the Moonlight Maze, which was said to have been deployed to probe government and institutions of higher education computer systems, but only in the United States. Then there was Code Red, which was deployed as a worm and utilized to launch denial of service attacks against the White House computer systems. Then Mountain View occurred, which resulted in unauthorized intrusion of United States municipal computer systems to compile information regarding utilities, data on government offices, and emergency systems. These cyberattack models are just a few of the most boggling efforts deployed in the 90s, by groups of hackers with personal agendas and bias motive to make some noise.

1.3 2000s

Unlike the 1990s, the new millennium ushered in some of the most malicious cyberattack events that forced an increase of cybersecurity leadership that resonates throughout 2023. First, in April 2000, Honorable Thomas M. Davis published a Congressional Record titled *Introduction of the Cybersecurity Information Act of 2000*, to introduce legislation with the significance for rendering increased focus and awareness of the nation's critical infrastructure and the threats and vulnerabilities engulfed in software, hardware, and the dependence of information systems and information technology for federal government purposes. [5] This Congressional Record was vital in making aware the controlling magnitude of strength the private sector embodied as it pertains to usage and reliance on information systems, information technology, cloud, and software and hardware for business, nonprofit, and academic purposes. Yet the entanglement of the private and public sector invoked a need to reassess the partnership and gain knowledge about the threats and vulnerabilities, and how these threats and vulnerabilities impact both sectors. Given there was a minimum number of qualified, educated, and skilled information systems and information technology practitioners in the 2000s, who could stand up and speak out about the issues the world faced in the new era of information technology and information systems. This increased concerns enveloping everyone from the White House administration to Deans and Department Directors of academia, who, too, wrestled to define curriculum and instruction to better prepare the next generation of information systems and information technology practitioners, to defend and protect the national critical infrastructure from adversarial attack agents.

Research compiled from Davis's Congressional Report explains that usage of technology by public and private sector increases risk because the same threats and vulnerabilities that the public sector faces also are faced by the private sector. Davis's Congressional Report expresses that computer networks are gateways that enable unauthorized access to sensitive government information from external attackers deriving from internal locations, particularly when such networks are not effectively assessed and secured. This Congressional Report also pointed out that the Presidential Decision Directive 63, published in May 1998, as well as the President's National Plan for Information Systems Security published in January 2000, invoked legislation to define reliable framework that would be instrumental in encouraging public and private sector to effectively discuss cybersecurity threats with the nation's private sector. Doing so was a dynamic way of increasing partnerships that helped bridge the line of communication and helped make both public and private sector aware of new attack methods and strategies that should be considered harmful enough to invoke sincere interest in helping thwart and deter these malicious acts of terror.

Davis was sure to mention the incident when Pan Am Sat's Galaxy IV satellite's onboard controllers were without service. The impact of this incident caused an estimated 75% or more of the nation's belt clip pagers to be inoperable, which caused hospitals tremendous worry because doctors and medical staff were unable to be reached for emergency purposes. This also created a problem for credit card consumers to make payments using their cards at retailers and gas pumps. Of course, through the years, changes were introduced that helped modify how cyberattack incidents are reported by both public and private sector. This also was a reason behind Thomas M. Davis's introduction of a Bill that invoked interest and gain support to secure information assets and protect the exchange of any information asset engulfing details about cybersecurity problems, resolutions, innovative text practices and results, as well as correlating issues regarding critical infrastructure security. This Bill encompassed details regarding the National Plan for Information Systems Protection, which was an invitation to dialogue published by the President of the United States on January 7, 2000, requesting all government bodies to implement modifications to all applicable laws regarding freedom of information, matters of liability, and antitrust.

Not soon after, this Bill and the National Plan for Information Systems became the gateway of fostering the technology and nontechnology industry-wide organizational infrastructure for information sharing and data analysis. One of the most outstanding components conveyed in this Bill is Article 1, Sec. 8, clause 3 of the Constitution of the United States supporting this new Act, which was to promote increased awareness of cybersecurity issues that target the nation's public and private sector, and to promote genuine concern for the privacy rights bestowed unto all American citizens. Most importantly, this Bill's purpose was to increase the government's responsibility to protect the private sector from cybercrime victimization and victimization from Internet service providers (ISPs), who would go on and play a role in supporting the usage of consumer's personal information for monetary gain, without concern of the impact. This Bill certainly was not the starting point of federal law and policy for the establishment of cybersecurity and cybersecurity leadership. After all, the Telecommunication Act passed in 1996, was an amendment of the Communications Act that encompassed the protection of private data and introduced data security requirements on any type of service provider rendering telephone and telegraph services but excluded radio and television broadcast networks as well as providers of broadband Internet services. [6]

Due to the growing central phenomenon of cyberattack incidents during the early 2000s, including cyber warfare, cyberspace spy tactics, and an ongoing concern regarding consumers' privacy rights, new legislation was introduced. Research compiled from the *Journal of National Security Law and Policy* reports that experiences enveloping Year 2000 millennium software issues, were incredibly important enough to ignite the government to build stronger trust alliances with private sector entities to implement stringent methodologies for controlling and managing risk woven in the information systems and information technology tools relied on by public and private sector. Thus, the National Institute of Standards and Technology grew to became instrumental in helping provide recommendations and guidelines to support vulnerabilities of federal information systems and usage of information technology for federal data storage. Then in 2002, Congress introduced legislation that helped usher in the enactment of the Federal Information Systems Management Act, empowering the National Institute of Standards and Technology to become an authority of security mechanisms, tools, and strategies the public and private sector could rely on, as trusted guidelines and recommendations for effective protection of sensitive data assets and technology tools. Soon after, legislation gained wide-spread authority to influence how risk management efforts, strategies, and methods, would be applied to federal information systems, as well as introduced theory regarding auditing of these systems. This helped determine when auditing should be implemented, how auditing should be assessed and updated, as well as who should be responsible to deploy audits; how an audit should be deployed and recorded, how to report audit results, and how often audits must be done. [7]

The development of cybersecurity in the United States empowered and informed international allies, including EU, United Nations, China, Soviet Union, and the Middle East, to invest more time understanding the climate of cybercrime and the impact this malicious and often heartless act of crime has on public and private sector entities and citizens. However, the brazing disregard for new legislation seems to empower cybercriminals to negate these efforts and continue introducing new methods and strategies of attack that undermined legal and policy regulations imposed, as well as seek new territories to continue deploying cyberattacks. This growth of awareness gained widespread attention, particularly when the UN General Assembly spoke up and shared publicly, that a proposed resolution to information security threats and concerns must be assessed annually. [8] In 2002, the rise of the cybersecurity culture resolution sponsored by the United States, correlated with the World Summit, enveloping Information Society and the International Telecommunications Union that helped create a model to increase end users' trust and confidence in usage of information communication technology. In fact, discussion grew rapidly in the UN General Assembly between 1998 and 2011, helping define authority for politico-military engagement to control security concerns in cyberspace, negating cybercrime as if it was different than the realm of cyberspace. This exposed the level of knowledge lacking outside the US; conveying how much countries and nation states were entangled in search for support on ideas to improve how they classify cyber incidents on land, air, sea, and space, as crimes that could be prosecuted under national and international law.

Furthermore, the UNGA was unsure how to define cybersecurity as a priority of national security, consistently wrestling to establish common ground among delegates grouped together as official authority regarding information security, i.e., UN Institute for Disarmament Research, the UN Global Alliance for ICT and Development, and the Internet Governance Forum. Additionally involved are 193 UN member states and 700 private companies and organizations. Unlike the United States, the UN's attempt to define cybersecurity met differences in knowledge of what encompassed cyber governance. While cyber domains were defined by the United States, i.e., sea, land, air, and space. The UN and others had not reached an understanding that enabled it to rest in creating legislation embodying various types of cybercrimes, including cyber terrorism, cyber bullying, cyber stalking, cyber espionage, and cyber warfare, as these subcategories have been introduced and categorized by threat level, and defined by meaning, purpose, tactics, and mitigation resolutions. Still efforts implemented by the UNGA and others were recognized in helping install a new approach to international security for telecommunications and information security.

Research also explains that the Russian Federation was the dominating UN member who ushered in the concept of international security, enveloping information security incidents. However, it is noted the United States was the first country that organized and implemented the framework to establish the embodiment of cybersecurity in 2002, and this framework became a dominating force by 2005. By 2006, several new sponsors joined forces with Russia and the United States on the definition of cybersecurity, which was to include critical information infrastructures. These sponsors included Armenia, Belarus, Chile, China, Ethiopia, Madagascar, Mali, Cuba, and Japan. By 2008, an additional 24 sponsors and co-sponsors joined, including

Brazil and Fiji. However, by 2011, many countries began withdrawing their support, leaving only 32 supporting countries. Thus, the final nine elements that cultivated what cybersecurity would encompass, includes awareness, accountability, response, ethics, democracy, risk assessment, security design and deployment, information security risk management, and auditing.

Today, a key element of cybersecurity is the CIA Triad, which embodies confidentiality, integrity, and availability. This ethic was framed by the Committee on National Security Systems (CNSS), which was previously known as the National Security Telecommunications and Information Systems Security Committee and was chaired by the U.S. Secretary of Defense. [9] In 2009, the Cyberspace Policy Review enforced the significance of an international governance of regulation to encompass information security in a language that could be applied universally and decrease the limited sharing of information regarding cybercrime incidents. This approach was beneficial because it enabled all countries and nation state members to have current trends in information about the type of cyberattacks deployed, methods of attack, and mitigation strategies being deployed, to deter successful attacks from impeding on organizations and government's ability to thwart serious security matters that could impact the economy and create havoc in business operations and communication.

By April 2008, it was validated that cybersecurity enveloped a taxonomy regarding all security matters to embody the compilation of tools, policies, perspectives of security, security strategies, recommendations and guidelines, risk management practices, efforts, best approaches, and information assurance, engulfing technologies which could be utilized to secure cyber domains and any organization's information assets and technologies, as well as individual's assets. However, efforts were being implemented to define a clear understanding of cybersecurity and how to define, assess, develop, implement, train others about the subject of cybersecurity, and how to define laws, regulations, and policy that would become instrumental in helping decrease threats and vulnerabilities. There remained a divide between the public and private sector. This divide created a wall of miscommunication. Private sectors were not so quick to share information about their cyberattack incidents because widespread news of such would impact their reputation. So, many private sector entities kept their successful cyberattack victimization incidents hidden. These actions helped cybercriminals continue integrating new methods of attack that were unexplainable and incapable of being thwart and deterred successfully.

In 2013, the development and introduction of the European Crime Center at Europol helped define the largest security organization, i.e., the

Organization for Security and Cooperation in Europe, which embodied 56 European states, Central Asia, and North America, including Romania, which, too, adopted cybersecurity definitions and purpose. [10] This established the development of the public and private sector relationship regarding cybersecurity and related matters of information security, as a new focus of national defense in protecting the information systems and technology of both government and private sector entities from cyberattacks and cybercrime victimization. Once the EU adopted the directive, it enacted the obligation for private sector to report all cyber incidents. Soon after, the United States introduced legislation requiring private sector organizations, including financial sector to report successful cyberattack incidents. In fact, in 2016, the Presidential Policy Directive (PPD), regarding the United States Cyber Incident Coordination, introduced a framework enforcing private sector entities to willfully report all cyber incidents once they are discovered. Later this same year, the European Union enacted the General Data Protection Regulation, to protect private citizen's personal data. This enacted legislation is now a highly respected controlling risk management factor globally.

The scope of the PPD established principles the federal government and private sector entities must adhere to, to build a foundation of trust and provide Americans the confidence that their privacy on the Internet and through usage of information communication technology (ICT) is a precedent of government law and policy. As a result, the meaning of cyber incident, is any unauthorized access of information system, information technology, or computer network hosting sensitive private information belonging to private or government persons, entities, or organizations, as well as any threat to the CIA triad, i.e., confidentiality, integrity, and availability of information assets, communication systems, or networks, including physical or virtual systems. [11] A significant cyber incident involves a malicious act of causing tremendous catastrophic harm to government or nongovernment information systems or property integrated with computer software and hardware, and causes harm to national security, foreign partnerships, the US economy, public trust, civil liberties, or public safety. However, the United States grew to become a pioneer in shifting how cyber incidents were to be assessed and managed under new federal laws and policy. In 2015, President Xi spoke at the World Internet Conference in Wuzhen, China, expressing his ideology of the meaning of cyber sovereignty, which he believed requires respecting another country's right to make their own policies and laws regarding the management of Internet accessibility and crime activity governance. [12] Then in 2017, Brad Smith, Chief Legal Officer of Microsoft spoke at a cybersecurity conference hoping to invoke a Digital Geneva Conference to call for action to empower governments to increase protection for civilians from being victimized by cyberattack and cybercrime activities. Smith strongly advocated that the private sector are sole owners of the Internet, and utilization of this open-source gateway connects them to their social communication and should be provided full priority in helping deter successful attacks from impeding on their privacy. Smith also believed that private sector citizens should be required to work in partnership with government entities to reduce the growing number of successful cyberattacks and cyber incidents. Not soon after was the creation of the vulnerabilities equities process, which is a methodology utilized by the federal government to determine at what point should they be required to share vulnerabilities with the private sector or decide to hold such information as intelligence and only render this data to Top Secret clearance holders.

However, the Obama Administration is noted for implementing efforts to improve the relationship between public and private sector. This approach was well received by many. Many cyber report incident websites grew over the eight-year timeline President Obama was in office. Then in 2018, President Donald Trump signed the updated revised edition of the National Cyber Strategy of the United States of America. This 27-page document provided Americans and the world, clarity, ensuring cyberspace is a top priority, as well as the security and safety of the American people. This document reports that Executive Order 13800 is introduced to increase the strength of cybersecurity correlating with federal networks and critical infrastructure. [13] This document also conveys that it was the focus of the Trump Administration to effectively deploy mitigation strategies to defend Americans by protecting networks, systems, functions, and data, as well as to promote prosperity for all Americans and foster enhanced domestic creativity. The Trump Administration also sought to deter successful cyberattacks and prosecute those found guilty of committing cyberattacks and cybercrimes, no matter what extent those crimes or attacks are. Most importantly, the Trump Administration sought to enforce an open and secure interoperable and reliable, secure Internet. The National Cyber Strategy ushered in a four-pillar infrastructure encompassing implementation efforts to increase protection for the American people, Homeland, and the American way of life. This includes securing federal networks and critical infrastructure, securing information, and combating cybercrime through improved methods of reporting cyber incidents. This also includes promoting American prosperity and fostering a vibrant and resilient digital economy, protecting Americans' innovative creativity and intellectual property rights, as well as thriving to increase development of an effective cybersecurity workforce. The third pillar encompassed preserving peace by increasing the strength of Americans; this includes increasing cyber stability via traditional state behavior, and deterring malicious acts of terror deployed through cyberspace. Pillar 4 focuses on expediting America's influence across the globe regarding cyberspace and protecting and promoting a secure Internet.

Cybersecurity leadership plays a role in how new federal legislation enacted in America and around the world, impacts human behavior correlating with cyberattack incidents. While more than 46 countries have enacted cybersecurity policy as a strategy to deter successful cyberattacks, there remains some countries that oppose America's and the EU's initiatives to build a stronger alliance to help protect public and private sector from cybercrime and cyberattack victimization. The United National Conference on Trade and Development reports that 80% of countries have enacted cybercrime legislation. The [14] will be moved to the end of the sentence regarding- 80% of countries have enacted cybercrime legislation. One of the most effective methods of cybersecurity leadership is deterrence. Deterrence can decrease the number of successful cyberattacks.

Research conveys that deterrence helps nations evade wars as well as the escalation of war. Deterrence enables national security to achieve long- and short-term goals. [15] Two primary purposes of deterrence are denial, which is the intent to frighten attackers from retaliatory aggression to defeat strong defense and resilience abilities, and punishment. Publishment enables national security to leverage the impact of deterrence and create a stabilized union of terror. With the use of deterrence, cybersecurity leadership establishes policy regulating what must be done to maintain the highest level of security, internally and externally, as well as creates a framework for organizational risk management infrastructure, to protect information assets, information systems, information technology, artificial intelligence automation, cloud services, infrastructure, and platforms. Deterrence implemented effectively can lower vulnerabilities and thwart successful cyberattack incidents from becoming major threats and impeding on the reputation of an organization.

Research conveys that deterrence must be assessed and implemented at each cyber domain level, i.e., land, air, sea, and space, to be successful. Research also reports that deterrence deployed using both denial and punishment, is often unsuccessful in deterring successful cyberattacks. Because cyber attackers are often deploying attacks offshore and/or internationally, legally, domestic law enforcement is not able to arrest suspects because of jurisdiction laws and regulations. One way cybersecurity leadership has helped modify this issue is by fostering partnerships with international law enforcement to enact laws that can be applied in those geographical locations, and culprits found guilty of cybercrimes in one country, deployed against another, will be required to serve a lengthy sentence in both the location the crime was deployed from and the location the crime took place. While there remains a slow progress of getting everyone onboard with this approach, efforts continue being implemented.

The psychology behind cybersecurity leadership proves that there has been some neglect in corporate and organizational settings. This impedes the ability to effectively assess how humans respond to cyberattacks physically, compared to how they respond virtually. Unless the cyberattack results in severe or catastrophic outcomes, victims of cybercrime incidents often are not as alarmed by these attacks because the damage is minimum. If a cyberattack is successful and causes tremendous financial or reputational damage to an organization or corporation, the outcome forces organizations to report the attack. Only then are humans made aware of these attacks and the damage that resulted from these attacks.

For example, in 2017, one of the largest cyberattacks deployed targeted Equifax, the international credit bureau corporation. The result of this attack was phenomenal because 145 million humans were victimized by inclusion, i.e., their personal information was stolen during the attack. The Gramm–Leach–Bliley Act was enacted in 1999, to require credit bureau reporting agencies to safeguard consumers' personal information. This Act continues to play a significant role in protecting citizens from cybercrime incident victimization, which is often due to internal human error incidents deployed within financial corporations, including credit reporting agencies. [16] Human error often leads to successful cyberattack incidents, particularly financial corporate settings. In fact, the establishment of the Consumer Financial Protection Bureau, in 2010, in correlation with the Dodd Frank Act, invoked credit reporting agencies to face tremendous scrutiny regarding their information security practices. Ineffective cybersecurity leadership within these corporations continue supporting successful unauthorized intrusion of information systems and networks, which are host to sensitive personal information regarding consumers.

Thus, cybersecurity leadership for healthcare organizations and institutions of higher education must be defined by the current and past legislation enacted as well as recommendations and guidelines provided by the National Institute of Standards and Technology. Maintaining alignment with these federal level regulatory and law practices, enables both corporations and organizations to establish standards within their environments that have come to be respected and trusted as methods of deterrence. This has also enabled improvement of cybersecurity policy compliance in corporate workplaces and organizational settings. Most importantly, this has ushered in a bridge of communication sharing regarding the method of attack deployed toward targets of cybercrime incidents. The ongoing level of communication shared between organizations enables the public and private sector to build firmer alliances that eases the ability to bring to justice those discovered engaging in cybercrime incidents, targeting financial institutions, healthcare organizations, and institutions of higher education. After all, the introduction of NIST SP 800-53 Rev.3 correlating protection of federal information systems and organizations, holds these sectors accountable because financial institutions receive federal guaranteed insurance on consumer financial accounts, healthcare organizations receive both federal and state funding, as well as institutions of higher education. While the National Institute of Standards and Technology revised and retired NIST SP 800-53 Rev. 3 on April 30, 2014, it was met with a new revision under NIST SP 800-53 Rev. 5 under Security and Privacy Controls for Information Systems and Organizations. [17]

Clearly, cybersecurity leadership requires an ongoing effort to stay current with trends in the industry, and globally, regarding cyberattack methods and strategies. Doing so enables federal and international lawmakers and policy makers to revise policies and laws that are outdated and cannot align with the type of incidents being deployed. This helps enforce previous enacted laws, giving them power to hold cybercriminals accountable, both domestically and internationally. Therefore, cybersecurity leadership must continue evolving with trends in cyberattacks, cybercrime, and cyber warfare, targeting government and business entities. Otherwise, the seemingly endless war against cybercriminals will never be won because cybercriminals seem to stay steps ahead of the lack of effective cybersecurity leadership.

1.4 2023 and Beyond 2024

To effectively assess the impact of cybersecurity leadership in 2023 required understanding the type of cybercrime incidents deployed, and the federal laws and policy enacted in public and private sectors, in 2023, to deter future cybercrime beyond 2024. Conducting such an assessment enables us to better understand what to expect beyond 2024. One type of cybercrime often perpetrated in 2023, was ransomware attacks. Research explains that the number of successful ransomware attacks deployed in 2021 and 2022 does not compare to the number of attacks deployed in 2023. There was a 94% increase of ransomware attacks. While an estimated 36% of ransomware attack victims were targeted successfully, due to vulnerabilities integrated in software applications relied on for business and government purposes. [18] The average estimated cost of a successful ransomware attack was $1.8 million, while global estimated cost reached $4.3 million. Ideally, one of the most recognized security applications implemented to increase deterrence of successful cyberattacks involving ransomware, is usage of artificial intelligence automation. IBM conveyed that usage of AI for security and automation reduces the overall cost for government and business organizations by $1.76 million. [19]

Thus, compiling research that educates cybersecurity leaders on what steps to take to effectively decrease ransomware cyberattacks and cybercrimes, beyond 2023 and 2024, provides clarity to improve methods of mitigation. Since it is reported publicly that successful ransomware attacks exploited known vulnerabilities, it is beneficial to increase auditing of all software applications utilized in all sectors; specifically, healthcare organizations and institutions of higher education. But this awareness is not new. In fact, usage of the U.S. Department of Defense public accessible website – Common Exposures and Vulnerabilities (CVE.org) – enables laypersons to understand the vulnerabilities woven in software applications utilized. Due to the growth of ransomware attacks deployed in 2023, it is obvious there is an increase of ineffective cybersecurity leadership in public and private sector. Perhaps this ineffectiveness is due to the inability to hire qualified cybersecurity leaders, information systems, and information technology practitioners. Perhaps this is due to an inability to hire trained and educated practitioners who have been made aware of the known vulnerabilities integrated in software applications utilized in workplaces. But no matter the cause, the effect of dealing with this problem is vital to aligning usage and reliance on technology tools and applications, with industry and manufacturer's recommendations and guidelines, regarding the upkeep and configuration of software applications relied on, to effectively secure them, which helps thwart the ability to exploit them. This is an effective deterrence.

For example, the list of successful ransomware attacks deployed in 2023 includes the Dish Ransomware attack, which was reported publicly after end users of Dish Network services began calling service centers reporting increased outages. This attack involved disruption of Dish website services, technology communication tools, and applets. The second alarming ransomware attack deployed, targeted financial firm NCR. This attack resulted in disruption of payment processing systems. However, it was not reported that consumers' personal information was stolen. The success rate of this attack impacts an increase of trust shared by consumers. Another alarming ransomware attack that occurred in 2023 was against the City of Dallas Texas. This attack focused on network printers, which are commonly embedded with Internet of Things (IoT) operating system applications and is the most misunderstood gateway of attack mode. As a result of this attack, the City of Dallas incurred a record number of data breaches across several platforms, including customer service apps, court records, water utilities, medical record information, and confiscation of countless government documents. One other alarming ransomware attack involved Sony. Research shows 3.14 GB of uncompressed data was stolen, and hackers tried obtaining a ransom for $2.5 million.

Thus, to prepare beyond 2024, recommendations and guidelines for public and private sector must involve increased cybersecurity leadership. It should not just improve awareness training but improve cybersecurity compliance with workplace information security policy, and improve alignment with federal laws, domestically and internationally. The growth of ransomware attacks does not seem to be coming near its end. After all, these attacks continue escalating. The future forecast of ransomware attacks will continue becoming sophisticated enough to outthink current applications of deterrence. One way to overcome this attack method is effectively assessing and auditing all software applications relied on for communication and business information system usage tools. Regardless of the inexperience of practitioners, organizations human resource managers and executive leaders need to become better informed and trained about cybersecurity. Effective cybersecurity must be a team effort. All personnel from executive leadership to customer service personnel, must be provided with continued training that prepares them to thwart successful exploitation of the software applications relied on. This training must include awareness of methods of attack, including phishing, whaling, and social engineering. This also must include providing knowledge of the type of federal and state laws personnel are held accountable to. Attack drills must be implemented to reinforce models of deterrence. Otherwise, the success of ransomware hackers will reach staggering heights, and businesses, governments, and organizations will continue being victimized and their deterrence efforts considered a waste of time.

1.5 Summary

Cybersecurity has established a gateway of knowledge sharing spanning the globe, reaching all cultures, and is interpreted by different languages. However, the meaning of cybersecurity has the same effect when deployed, audited, assessed, and misunderstood. Despite government efforts to increase federal and state laws and policy to improve methods of deterrence, cybercriminals increase their knowledge of attack methods and seem to outsmart the strategies of deterrence implemented by government and private sector. The aggressive and arrogant attitude of cybercriminals proves a level of disregard for authority and reveals a disrespect for human dignity, integrity, and trust in a system defined by rules and regulations, implemented and enforced to protect the privacy of all humans and their personal information assets. This scale of arrogance must endure a retaliation of criminal prosecution that represents how victims feel and the dollar amount invested to continue increasing the scale of security methods and practices deployed to protect information assets and human privacy rights. Cybersecurity leadership is a way of redefining how regulations and communication shared between public and private sector is governed. However, unless there is a drive to enforce compliance with systematic authority for usage of technology tools and applications in both public and private sector entities, the investment of cybersecurity becomes null.

In addition, it is obvious the world faces a tremendous war enveloping information sharing, development, and security. It is obvious the threat of insecure information systems plays a role in how information assets are secured and accessed. It does not matter if the hosting of information assets is by government or business, organizations, or individuals. It is clear that the message of cybersecurity continues to be ignored by the masses, including the public and private sector. Legislation continues implementing as much deterrence efforts as possible via the number of new laws and policies enacted. But without compliance and respect for these legislative practices and systems of risk management control, the impact of these efforts remains absent. Furthermore, despite the efforts implemented by legal agencies, the number of successful attacks deployed as ransomware proves hackers and cybercriminals are less concerned with the fear of being caught. In fact, the consistent bravery of cybercriminals imposing their efforts on public and private sector, privacy, and security controls, conveys a nonchalant ideology for the existence of cybersecurity and cybersecurity leadership.

Thus, when considering the role cybersecurity leadership plays in helping healthcare organizations and institutions of higher education avoid victimization of cybercrime, where do we begin to establish trust in our cybersecurity leaders, information systems, and information technology practitioners. Overcoming the misunderstanding of cybersecurity and its significance will take continued efforts by all; not just public and private sector entities but citizens, who are commonly the victim of cyberattacks. But this message isn't new. We have been talking about this subject since the new millennium began. That was 24 years ago. Twenty-four years to date, we still have a consistent absence of effectively trained cybersecurity practitioners. Those currently managing information technology and information system, roles and responsibilities, are often the same ones filling cybersecurity roles. The lack of effective and efficient training of these personnel members can be one problem. The whole problem does not root itself in just a lack of knowledge. The system itself is a problem. First, technology hardware and software developers must increase their implementation of improved security applications that help deter a successful attack of their applications. Knowing system vulnerabilities exist requires deployment of effective security control. When cybercriminals can research a database to learn the known vulnerabilities of any software application, and risk management is not applied to patch such vulnerabilities, the blame falls on the software developer, not the end user. Thus, legislation needs to engulf accountability on the manufacturers providing the software applications utilized by public and private sectors. Meanwhile, when end users are not maintaining the compliance risk management control recommended by the manufacturer, the end user is responsible for the ease of attack method. This is how exploits occur. Unless the partnership between manufacturer and end user improves, the scale of cybersecurity implemented will remain ineffective.

Furthermore, unless executive leaders are provided knowledge of the significance of increasing usage of security control applications, i.e., new software applications woven with artificial intelligence, there will remain insecurities within that information system and the alignment of usage with information technology. In fact, IBM reported that usage of artificial intelligence automation can be instrumental in decreasing the number of successful cyberattacks. But unless those managing information systems and information technology are knowledgeable of these facts, sadly, their workplace will continue being targets of victimization. Thus, to improve knowledge sharing, this chapter was an entrance point preparing you for what this book represents and embody. The learning experience will help you define improved strategies to effectively assess the software applications relied on for your entity's purposes, be it business, government, or nonprofit. Having access to information that prepares you to avoid victimization can be instrumental in improving current trends in your information system and information technology risk management. Therefore, it is the intent to share all that has been researched regarding cybersecurity and the trends in healthcare organizations and institutions of higher education, cybercrime, and cyberattack incidents. Despite the efforts of cybercriminals, this war targeting your entity's information systems, networks, and information technology, is one you can win but with a team effort. Beware of the enemy that seeks to exploit the vulnerabilities woven in the applications relied on for communication and business purposes. Those we commonly place trust in can be the very ones to attack us. Therefore, staying aware of new methods of deterrence will be your best method of deterrence. Connecting with networks of cybersecurity organizations and associations is key. Partnering with institutions of higher education is proven to be worth rendering qualified practitioners, and it will enable both public and private sector to continue building teams of experts that are working together to defeat cybercriminals and their attack modes. Knowing who to turn to and who to trust will be a deterrence strategy in 2024 and beyond.

This educational tool shares increased hands-on practices using some of the best software applications relied on today for cybersecurity. Learning how to understand these tools is the first step in effective cybersecurity leadership. Knowing why these tools exist and how to effectively review and audit these tools, is another step in effective cybersecurity leadership. Working in partnership with manufacturers of any tool relied on is another key. Taking these steps to acquire this knowledge proves you are searching for improvement. Thus, this book is an answer to many of your concerns and questions.

In fact, Chapter 2 will provide knowledge regarding cybersecurity leadership for healthcare organizations. You will learn about current trends of cybersecurity leadership impacting healthcare organizations. You will also become aware of the method of assessing, developing, implementing, and managing cybersecurity leadership for healthcare organizations. In summary, you will reiterate your learning experience and review an investigative scenario, as well as complete discussion questions to help reinforce your comprehension.

1.6 Investigative Scenario

The central phenomenon enveloping ransomware attack methods continues escalating, to a point nation leaders fear a catastrophic event that will cripple the economy. Satellite Internet access is becoming a growing norm in many countries, making it easier for cybercriminals to partner with private sector service providing corporations, who render website connectivity, mobile phone communication, and processing of Internet orders through virtual payment processing systems that transmit through satellite connectivity. Although authority enacts laws and policy to control risk and malicious acts of terror deployed through usage of Internet connectivity and technology tools and devices, such laws are limited. In 2024, new attack methods will alter what has helped previously define attack methods and how to define deterrence strategies. A successful ransomware attack could wipe out financial institutions in Switzerland, but this only impacts consumers who rely on those services. When the ransomware threat gains access to Top level secrets of adversaries and vice versa, the retaliation impact could be as rememberable as the Ukraine and Russia war. The impact will define how nations partner to improve methods of deterrence unknown today. Why do we wait until attacks are successful before we plan to secure the infrastructures, services, platforms, networks, systems, artificial intelligence botnets, and information technology? If we have learned anything, cybercriminals are not ceasing their malicious activities. Thus, the world is in trouble. One way to redefine methods that are effective is defining a system of cybersecurity leaders, who are committed and driven to stay informed, is building a network of information sharing. Such a system of data sharing can improve stability and mitigation strategies to defeat ransomware attackers. Knowing what steps to take to implement control of risk, audit vulnerabilities in software, and manage human error, must be top priority. But there are other actions, strategies, methods, policies, and ideas that you have that could support a new model of cybersecurity leadership for healthcare organizations and institutions of higher education. I'm interested in what your research finds. Please consider taking part in an international cybersecurity leadership and policy council focused on cybersecurity leadership and methods of effective implementation and management of cybersecurity policy. This council enables you to share research on these issues and begin helping others define a method of cybersecurity leadership that is universally understood. You can provide your research response on this subject and share it with Dr. Bradley Fowler, to be considered for adoption in future research projects with Dr. Fowler. Submit your response to bfowler@captechu.edu. Be sure to add the key phrase: Chapter 1 investigative scenario | future research response.

1.7 Discussion Questions

1. What branches of federal law worked in concert with United States Congress to enact laws defining how government, businesses, and citizens must act to respond to cyber activities deployed across the Internet?
2. Why was the General Data Protection Regulation enacted?
3. What attack mode ushered in an increased awareness to make cybersecurity a precedence to control cybercriminal activity?
4. What year did the Congressional legislation usher in the enactment of the Federal Information Systems Management Act to empower the

National Institute of Standards and Technology to become an authority of security mechanisms?

5. What was validated in 2008 ensuring cybersecurity encompassed control of security matters?
6. What helps nations evade war as well as the escalation of war?
7. How can cybersecurity leaders understand software application vulnerabilities?
8. What NIST special publication explains Security and Privacy Control for Information Systems and Organizations?
9. What city government faced the rememberable ransomware attack in 2023?
10. Who reported that 80% of countries have enacted cybercrime legislation in 2023?

Glossary

Brain virus – released in 1986 impacting IBM personal computers and compatibles, resulting in the replacement of the boot sector of a floppy disk with a virus edition. Used to infect floppy disk speed, making kilobytes of saved data inaccessible.

Distributed denial of service attack – a method of attack that floods a web interface to prevent end users access to the web page content delivery.

Executable code – created to cause a computer to perform specific tasks, also known as machine code.

Morris worm – oldest computer worm resulting in the first felony conviction in the United States under the 1986 Computer Fraud and Abuse Act, used to exploit vulnerabilities in Unix sendmail program, acting as a buffer overflow, and exploit weaknesses in passwords.

Phishing – transmission of fraudulent communication appearing to be from a legitimate sender or reputable source, used to gain access to sensitive information to steal money and defraud by confiscating login information, or install malware on a victim's device, i.e., mobile, desktop, laptop.

Sputnik – satellite launched by the Soviet Union in 1957 to send radio signal back to earth; considered an effective tool for listening to conversations from space and sending messages back to earth in radio sound waves.

Social engineering – deception used to manipulate individuals into sharing their personal data and confidential information that is often used for fraudulent purposes.

Ransomware attack – malware deployed to attain monetary payment to remove the malware installed on a device without permission.

Whaling – targeting corporate executive leaders as a reputable constitute, to gain access to sensitive information that could lead to a cyber-criminal gaining access to corporate secrets, personnel's identifiable credentials, and/or financial records and information.

References

[1] Rudu, R. (2013, July 11). Negotiating Meanings for Security in The Cyberspace. [PDF] Retrieved from: https://www.researchgate.net/publication/255697155_Negotiating_meanings_for_security_in_the_cyberspace

[2] Arciola, R. (2022, April 12). Computer Viruses of the 80s and early 90s- A trip through memory lane. [Website] Retrieved from: https://linkedin.com/pulse/computer-viruses-80s-early-90s-trip-through-memory-lane-arciola#:~:text=The%20Brain%20Virus%20(1986)%20-,the%20first%20

[3] International Telecommunication Union, (n.d.) National Security for Information Security in the Slovak Republic. [PDF] Retrieved from: http://itu.int/en/ITU-D/Cybersecurity/Documents/National_Strategies_Repository/Slovakia_2008_National_Strategy_for_ISEC.pdf

[4] Brown, G. & Poellet, K. (2012, October). The Customary International Law of Cyberspace. [PDF] Retrieved from: https://www.jstor.org/stable/26267265

[5] Davis, M.T. (2000, April 12). Introduction of the Cybersecurity Information Act 2000. [Website] Retrieved from: https://sgp.fas.org/congress/2000/cybersec.html

[6] Congressional Research Service, (2019, March 25). Data Protection Law: An Overview. [PDF] Retrieved from: https://crsreports.congress.gov/product/pdf/R/R45631

[7] Nojeim, T. G. (2010, August 13). Cybersecurity and Freedom on the Internet. [PDF] Retrieved from: https://archive.ccrvoices.org/cdn.agilitycms.com/centre-for-communication-rights/Images/Articles/pdf/Nojeim2010.pdf

[8] Rudu, R. (2013, July 11). Negotiating Meanings for Security in The Cyberspace. [PDF] Retrieved from: https://www.researchgate.net/

publication/255697155_Negotiating_meanings_for_security_in_the_cyberspace

[9] Whitman, E.M. & Mattord, J. H. (2017) Management of Information Security, (5th Ed), Cengage Learning, Boston, MA.

[10] Dumitru, D. & Cosmin, G. (n.d.) Cybersecurity-A New Dimension of National Defense. [PDF] Retrieved from: https://www.sweetstudy.com/files/cyber-security-a-new-dimensionofthenationaldefense-pdf

[11] The White House, (2016, July 26). Presidential Policy Directive-United States Cyber Incident Coordination. [Website] Retrieved from: https://obamawhitehouse.archives.gov/the-press-office/2016/07/26/presidential-policy-directive-united-states-cyber-incident

[12] Segal, A. (2017, December 21). Bridging the Cyberspace Gap-Washington and Silicon Valley. [PDF] Retrieved from: https://www.jstor.org/stable/26470519

[13] The White House, (2018, September). The National Cyber Strategy. [PDF] Retrieved from: https://trumpwhitehouse.archives.gov/wp-content/uploads/2018/09/National-Cyber-Strategy.pdf

[14] United Nations Conference on Trade and Development, (2023, December 24). Cybercrime Legislation Worldwide. [Website] Retrieved from: https://unctad.org/page/cybercrime-legislation-worldwide

[15] Chen, J. (2018). Effectively Exercising Deterrence in the Cyber Domain. [PDF] Retrieved from: https://www.proquest.com/conference-papers-proceedings/effectively-exercising-deterrence-cyber-domain/docview/2018924244/se-2

[16] Consumer Data Industry Association, (2023). Data Security Regulation of Consumer Reporting Agencies. [Website] Retrieved from: https://www.cdiaonline.org/resources/for-reporting-industry-professionals/data-security-regulation-of-consumer-reporting-agencies/

[17] National Institute of Standards and Technology, (2020, September). Security and Privacy Controls for Information Systems and Organizations. [Website] Retrieved from: https://csrc.nist.gov/pubs/sp/800/53/r5/upd1/final

[18] Technologies, S. (2023, December 21). A Comprehensive List of Top Ransomware Attacks in 2023. [Website] Retrieved from: https://www.sangfor.com/blog/cybersecurity/list-of-top-ransomware-attacks-in-2023

[19] IBM. (2023). Cost of a Data Breach Report 2023. [Website] Retrieved from: https://www.ibm.com/reports/data-breach

2

Cybersecurity Leadership for Healthcare Organizations

Learning Objectives

- Distinguish cybersecurity leadership for healthcare organizations.
- Distinguish current trends in healthcare organization cybersecurity issues.
- Assess and develop effective cybersecurity leadership planning and policy compliance.
- Articulate vendor management strategies for healthcare organizations.

2.1 Introduction

Healthcare organizations are consistently becoming a primary target of cyberattacks because they host patient information that remain unsecured in many hospitals, medical centers, clinics, and emergency care unit information systems. One reason why this phenomenon is growing is because there remains consistent neglect to align business operations with federal requirements and industry standardizations enacted under HIPAA laws. Such neglect invokes consumers to build a perception of distrust in how healthcare organizations store patient information as well as share information with third-party service providers and business partners. Unfortunately, for many healthcare organizations, the chief financial officer is chosen to make decisions regarding IT architecture. This decision-making involves determining what technology tools should be relied on and delivered through third-party service providers, who often fail to execute supporting cybersecurity services to ensure information assets belonging to healthcare organizations, are effectively stored and secured, without unauthorized contact from cyberattack agents. Moreover, research reports current EHR systems healthcare organizations are utilizing are outdated. [1] In many instances, in-house designed interface EHR systems have been outdated for years. This has created one of the biggest obstacles for defining a reliable and scalable EHR system. After all, implementing a new EHR results in quarterly training of personnel, i.e., physicians, nurses, and administrative staff. Training cannot be ignored. Training is essential in reducing human error. Human error in EHR systems create gateways for unauthorized intrusion in healthcare organization's information systems. Once hackers attain access and retrieve information assets, reputational damage is inflicted, often sending consumers to competitors for their medical and healthcare services and products. Thus, reliance on outdated EHR can result in IT support designated for various healthcare organization departments, i.e., nursing, pharmacy, laboratory, imaging, and risk management, to be limited. And although this does not impose a serious threat to some healthcare organization's ability to protect and secure patient information, this could impact the cost of care, especially if usage of the outdated system increases. In fact, too often, healthcare organization executive leaders are unaware of the impact old legacy systems have on finance and outputs. [2] Healthcare organization business leaders also neglect to comprehend how legacy systems can hinder their growth and increase risk of falling behind competitors. This leverage in technology usage enables competitors to win clients away from one healthcare entity to another. Therefore, clinging on to an outdated legacy system, increases cost, impacts the ability to maintain customers, risks the chance of losing employees, increases the risks of security breaches, and decreases the ability to scale up. This impedes on the ability of having the right equipment and digital assets to manage daily healthcare organization tasks effectively and securely.

2.2 Current Trends

One way to resolve this issue is integrating software to deliver automated management of organizational operations. Artificial intelligence has become an application of architected reliability, capable of meeting the needs of healthcare organizations. Usage of robotic processes enveloped in automation, increases effective management of administrative procedures, including information systems. AI operates like a human, deploying efforts defined by the script or input programmed in the operating system. This is an inexpensive method of integrating AI, and it is simple to configure for programming. AI requires workflow management, business rules, and provides a presentation layer woven in the information system. Since healthcare organizations require repetitive tasks management and efficiency, such as prior authorization to deploy efforts to update patient records or billing, AI can be beneficial in overseeing patient engagement. [3]

This chapter delivers distinguished knowledge regarding a proposed strategy for maintaining the information technology (IT) values needed for healthcare organizations, including a proposed healthcare information system solution, integrated through software and AI automation provided by Amazon Web Services (AWS), cloud security management console. AWS has introduced a three-tier cloud interface. This application supports patient care, decreases cost, and improves the outcome of patient–physician relationship. AWS Open EMR Cloud Express is a single server cloud capable of managing healthcare organization's long-term usage that renders low maintenance customizable installations that is cost effective. [4] AWS renders an application titled RedOx, which accelerates the exchange of healthcare, internally and externally, enabling patients to access their EHR in a cloud application. The enhanced layer of security in the cloud provides assurance that the data is encrypted and impenetrable from external cyberattack methods. Both human error and civil liabilities are reduced as well. AWS offers several use cases, including clinical information systems, health and disease prediction, healthcare analytics, healthcare compliance, healthcare datasets, interoperability, IT infrastructure, medical imaging, population health, security and data privacy, virtual care, and patient engagement. Healthcare organizations utilizing this method of IT infrastructure, will gain leverage to compete with competitors, and shift automation processing through AWS Sumo Logic software, which is a Software as a Service (SaaS) to determine baseline activity, reducing the time to investigate and correct security or operation concerns. Access to these applications is available in the AWS management console and can be configured to any healthcare organization's security needs.

Thus, it is essential healthcare organizations, their executive leadership, and IT practitioners, research how to upgrade to recommended healthcare information system applications, shared in this chapter. Doing so can improve strategic planning and development of third-party partnerships that help increase revenue. This can also help measure the effectiveness of implementing artificial intelligence. Furthermore, this will support configuring a baseline to measure activity on the network and virtual servers, to determine the level of security required to effectively deter a successful cyberattack incident. Throughout this chapter, you will be introduced to research compiled on Intermountain Healthcare. Intermountain Healthcare provides services and delivers products in Montana, Utah, Colorado, Nevada, Idaho, Kansas, and Wyoming. This nonprofit service provider offers hospital and healthcare for cancer, heart service, women's healthcare services, orthopedics, and pediatrics. Its primary headquarters is in Murray, Utah. Intermountain Health delivers 47 unique services and has over 10,000 employees. The 33-hospital system reported a 40% year-over-year increase in revenue earnings, reaching more than $3.9 billion between January and March 2023. Such an increase is accredited to the merger of eight hospitals previously known as Salt Lake City Health. [5] However, research reported in 2013, conveys Intermountain Health operating income fell by $26 million. The nature of this healthcare organization ranked as the 11th nonprofit healthcare system in the United States, includes delivering reliable and trusted services through clinics, medical groups, and insurance. Using this healthcare organization as an example, provides a clear assessment of how effective cybersecurity leadership must be in supporting healthcare organizations.

As you read and assess content in this chapter, you will distinguish the value of cybersecurity leadership for healthcare organizations. You will also review current trends in healthcare organizations' cybersecurity issues and assess how cybersecurity leadership should be integrated for healthcare organizations. You will develop effective planning for implementation and articulating management strategies for cybersecurity leadership, as well as review a summary to reiterate your learning comprehension. An investigative scenario helps you understand how significant your research and input is to the ongoing discussion of cybersecurity leadership for healthcare organizations. And discussion questions will help ensure your reading and knowledge attainment is memorable.

2.3 Assessing, Developing, Implementing, and Managing Cybersecurity Leadership

There is an increasing need for cybersecurity for healthcare organizations due to the growing number of successful cyberattack incidents reported over the last three years. Research reports an estimated 100 million people were victims of a cyberattack deployed against their healthcare organization in 2023. [6] In 2022, an estimated 44 million people were victims of cyberattack, involving the dissemination of their personal medical information on the dark web. This central phenomenon is not going to end any time soon. In fact, it is predicted that in 2024, the number of healthcare organizations experiencing cyberattack victimization will double that of 2022 and 2023. Thus, to help deter healthcare organizations from this threat of victimization, requires increased cybersecurity leadership, implemented with a sincere and honest method of deterrence that combat this act of attack deployed by attack agents. However, due to healthcare organization's dependence on third-party software applications that have also been targeted in cyberattacks, it is challenging to distinguish a reliable and trusted method of effectively securing these organizational information assets.

Some of the nation's largest healthcare organizations are solely reliant on outsourcing their information databases to third-party service providers. The current lists of known healthcare organizations that rely on third-party healthcare information system database service providers, who were successfully victimized in 2023, through hacking incidents, include:

- Postmeds, Inc. affected 2.5 million individuals' healthcare records.
- Western Washington Medical Group affected 350,000 individuals' healthcare records.
- Greater Rochester Independent Practice Association, Inc. affected 270,000 individuals' healthcare records.
- Radius Global Solutions affected 132,000 individuals' healthcare records.
- Dakota Eye Institute affected 100,000 individuals' healthcare records.
- Walmart Inc. Associated Health and Welfare Plan affected 85,000 individuals' healthcare records.
- Westat, Inc. affected 50,000 individuals' healthcare records.
- Brooklyn Premier Orthopedics affected 48,000 individuals' healthcare records.
- PeakMed affected 27,000 individuals' healthcare records.
- Hospital and Medical Foundation of Paris, Inc. affected 16,000 individuals' healthcare records.
- Frederick's Foot and Ankle Center, PLC. affected 14,000 individuals' healthcare records.
- Peerstar LLC. affected 11,000 individuals' healthcare records.
- Atlas Healthcare affected 10,000 individuals' healthcare records.

The *HIPAA Journal* reports that hacking was the typical approach to obtaining unauthorized entrance into these healthcare organization's information databases, accounting for an estimated 76% of attacks deployed in October 2023, accounting for 31 incidents, and 99% of the breached records stolen estimated at 3.5 million healthcare consumers and personnel. [7] The average data breach encompassing hacking incidents is 114,000 records, while the median data breach size recorded is 4000 records. Thus, to decrease the growing number of successful hacking incidents deployed against health-care organizations, research was compiled on Intermountain Healthcare, as a research study, to define an improved information database storage and usage application that also can be effective in decreasing successful cyberattacks. This research can be applied to healthcare organizations universally, but only if those healthcare organizations are willing to invest in upgrading their current information system, to the recommended guidelines and system shared in this research. This research identifies issues Intermountain Healthcare experienced due to a lack of usage of cloud computing architecture, as it relates to its current healthcare information system. This research outlines the essential activities needed to assess, develop, implement, and successfully secure the system development life cycle (SDLC) for Intermountain Healthcare information system. Additionally, this research shares the proposed healthcare information system's impact, relating to diversity, equity, and inclusion regarding healthcare provisions (e.g., access, cost, and quality). This research also provides a risk analysis strategy for Intermountain Healthcare usage of cloud computing as it aligns with applicable laws and standards enacted by Congress and enforced by the United States Department of Homeland Security, National Security Agency, the White House National Cyber Strategy, as well as The National Institute of Standards and Technology guidelines and recommendations. This research summarizes the best practices and policies for Intermountain Healthcare cloud computing architecture as it relates to data governance, information exchange, as well as technical and structural interoperability. This research estimates one thing that could go wrong in implementing this proposed healthcare information system and renders a strategic plan to ensure the success of cloud computing architecture implementation through vendor management and team management.

Intermountain Healthcare operates by delivering services and products in Montana, Utah, Colorado, Nevada, Idaho, Kansas, and Wyoming. This nonprofit service provider offers hospital and healthcare for cancer, heart healthcare services, women's healthcare services, orthopedics, and pediatrics. Its primary headquarters is in Murray, Utah. This healthcare organization delivers 47 unique services and has over 10,000 employees. The 33-hospital system reported a 40% year-over-year increase in revenue earnings, reaching more than $3.9 billion between January and March 2023. This increase in revenue is accredited to the merger of eight hospitals, previously known as Salt Lake City Health. [8] In 2023, research conveyed that Intermountain Health operating income fell by $26 million. The nature of the organization as the 11th nonprofit healthcare system in the United States, includes delivering reliable and trusted services through clinics, medical groups, and insurance. Research reports, their mission is to provide medical, dental, vision, short-term income protection, and basic and supplemental group term life insurance benefits for those eligible, either due to disability and/or retired employees, as well as their eligible dependents. [9]

The identified issues relating to the current information system relied on for billing and patient care, had known vulnerabilities integrated when research was conducted in 2023. Reports from the U.S. Department of Defense Common Exposure and Vulnerabilities website conveyed that Intermountain Health software applications had 27 known vulnerabilities in 2023, and experienced 136 overall vulnerabilities, since 2007. The publication of these vulnerabilities published on the CVE website, delivers a clear method for hackers to gain unauthorized entrance into these vulnerable systems. [10] Therefore, this creates the serious need to invest in a healthcare information system that can be hosted via cloud computing and decrease unauthorized access to sensitive data assets. One of the most effective service providers for cloud computing for healthcare organizations is Amazon Web Services, who provides elastic health records. This new approach enables health record systems to increase service demands for patients, clinicians, and the administrative business functions. [11]

The native AWS service groups-i.e., Elastic Compute Cloud, Elastic Block Store, Elastic File System, load balancing, IP address, Elastic Disaster Recovery, and Elastic Container Service, help to improve organizational transformation of elastic health records (EHR). In fact, the AWS elastic health record system encompasses an entire digital health ecosystem that encompasses radiology imaging, picture archiving and communication systems, document management systems, coding systems, lab systems, and blood bank systems, as well as historical records from previous EHRs, which are all enveloped with interface engines. This information system can be beneficial in supporting Intermountain Health or any healthcare organization, in deploying all applications in a private cloud. Doing so enables Intermountain Health or any healthcare organization, to rest assured that using this reliable and secure system is worthy of investment. In fact, research conveys that utilizing cloud for healthcare organizations, can increase storage management and increase protection of shared electronic health records, including laboratory information system, pharmacy information system, and medical imagery. [12]

Furthermore, research conveys that utilizing cloud computing helps patients improve their care, because cloud computing enables reliable up-to-date health records and provides continued interactions between many healthcare providers. However, since there is a lack of standards, regulations, and interoperability problems, the biggest issue has been the slow adoption of cloud usage by healthcare organizations, because of concerns regarding security, confidentiality as well as trust. In fact, the SDLC (software development life cycle) for cloud computing for electronic health records, include minimizing project risks by enforcing planning to ensure the software aligns with a healthcare organization's needs and expectations, both during production and beyond. This methodological approach must include a step-by-step strategy to divide the software development application process. [13] This is important because integrating a new SDLC can be challenging. However, if successfully deployed, this approach will enable an improved ability to develop, implement, and manage the applications required to meet the usage needs of any healthcare organization. The benefits utilizing this method and strategy also encompass improved visibility of the development lifecycle, creating improved efficiency estimation, as well as planning and effective scheduling. This helps increase risk management development, implementation, and manage cost estimation. Most importantly, this enables improved customer satisfaction.

Additionally, essential activities in the SDLC for cloud computing, include planning the new system, which often encompasses estimating tasks through the usage of a cost–benefit analysis, and effectively scheduling and estimating the required resources. This also requires the system development team to compile input from stakeholders, including internal and external experts, acquire feedback from patients, and feedback from clinicians, which can be useful in streamlining the creation for software requirement specifications. This also requires the team to effectively establish expectations and define goals that can enhance the project planning process. Next, it is important for the development team to design and implement the coded product to specification needs and test the system prior to full deployment. Of course, maintenance is the final phase, which requires the team to effectively fix the bugs, understand the significance of managing customer problems, and manage software modifications as the need occurs. This can invoke development teams to improve how they monitor system performance and can be instrumental in determining the level of security required, as well as assess how to effectively configure security correctly.

Using cloud computing architecture can impact an organization's ability to stay current in cloud trends and compete with competitors, who are already integrating diverse team actions in partnership with cloud practitioners. Cloud can also be beneficial in managing costs of services and product delivery. Utilizing cloud computing for billing and invoice generating and dissemination among physicians and patients is also a benefit. In fact, AWS confesses that it provides one of the most secure, reliable, and broadly adopted cloud platforms for healthcare providers, and is a dynamic application for protecting healthcare organization information worldwide. Healthcare organizations can accelerate innovation, unlock siloed data, and develop personalized care strategies – all while operating securely in a highly regulated industry. More importantly, AWS provides HIPAA-eligible services and certifications that meet the healthcare industry, global IT and compliance standards, such as GDPR (General Data Protection Regulations), HITRUST, and ISO 27001:2022.

As previously mentioned, the General Data Protection Regulation was enacted by the European Union in 2016 and has become a "Gold Standard" for managing the security and privacy of consumer data. This law superseded the 1995 Data Protection Directive. HITRUST was enacted as a blanket encompassing all cybersecurity laws and regulation under one roof, i.e., HIPAA, GDPR, PCI-DSS, etc. Healthcare organizations implementing this body of law can be ensured that they are conducting cybersecurity operations in alignment with top-tier cybersecurity laws enacted in the United States and EU. ISO 27001:2022 embody controls to effectively align cybersecurity, information security, and privacy protection. Although this body of regulation is industry organized and recognized, it is a framework that resonates across the information system and information technology industry.

Moreover, the most effective way to ensure integrity through the deployment of AWS services and infrastructure, is defining a clearly conveyed risk analysis strategy for Intermountain Healthcare usage and reliance of cloud computing, as it aligns with applicable laws and standards enacted by Congress and enforced by the U.S. Department of Homeland Security and National Security Agency, as well as the White House National Cyber Strategy. The National Institute of Standards and Technology developed special publications that offer recommended guidelines for effectively managing and securing cloud computing. Take for instance, NIST 800-146 Cloud Computing Synopsis and Recommendations, explains the value of cloud computing, but also provides information regarding general cloud environments, such as public cloud, hybrid cloud, and outsourced private cloud scenarios, which help healthcare organizations gain increased knowledge about issues that may arise, and how to respond to and adopt cloud for data asset storage and security. This special publication explains Infrastructure as a Service (IaaS), including a scope of control on software stack. This also conveys what the cloud manager role should encompass, and operations of the computer manager. Issues and concerns are discussed, including compatibility with legacy security vulnerabilities, verification of authenticity of the IaaS service provider, i.e., AWS, strategies for dynamic network configuration for providing isolation, as well as clarity regarding open issues. Open issues encompass latency, off-line data synchronization, scalable programming, and data storage management. [14]

Additionally, it is reported by the National Institute of Standards and Technology that risk management must be a cyclically executed process enveloped with a set of coordinated activities for managing and controlling risks. This method focuses on the enhancement of strategic and tactical security, and the execution of a risk assessment. This also includes details regarding the implementation of a risk mitigation strategy, and shares knowledge regarding the deployment of risk control techniques and procedures for continued monitoring of the information system. Cloud-based information systems, aligned with traditional information systems, also require risk management that is effectively managed throughout the information system development life cycle (SDLC).

Interestingly, while cloud computing can be a benefit for Intermountain Health or any healthcare organization, it is important that Intermountain Health and other healthcare organizations, align business practices with the policy recommendations and laws enacted, including HIPAA, and those previously mentioned. However, when focusing on data governance, it is important that healthcare organizations also adhere to NIST SP 800-53 Rev. 5, which focuses on security and privacy controls for information systems and organizations. This policy will enable healthcare organizations to establish a clearly written catalog of security and privacy controls for information systems and protect organizational operations and assets from a diverse set of threats and risks, including hostile attacks, human errors, natural disasters, structural failures, foreign intelligence entities, and privacy risks. These strategy controls are flexible and customizable and can be deployed as part of an organization-wide process to manage risk. This also helps control diverse requirements derived from mission and business needs, including the laws, executive orders, directives, regulations, policies, standards, and guidelines.

Furthermore, NIST delivers recommendations regarding information exchange in special publication 800-47 titled *Managing the Security of Information Exchange*, which conveys in part, that the protection of the information exchanged or accessed before, during, and after the exchange, and that provides guidance on identifying information exchanges, considerations for protecting exchanged information, and the agreement(s) required to help manage the risk associated with exchanging information, is vital when using cloud computing. [15] Relying on these recommendations and guidelines will help Intermountain Health and other healthcare organizations, define the scope of their information exchange, understand the benefits of utilizing a secure management of information exchange; identify types of information exchange, and learn more about the potential security risks that correlate with information exchange. This helps improve how healthcare organizations apply these methods with their mission and business needs, to effectively exchange information securely. [16]

Additionally, it is important that Intermountain Health and other healthcare organizations understand that cloud computing for healthcare organizations and the healthcare industry, is expected to grow up to $50 billion domestically, annually, by 2025. However, examining the benefits of cloud computing architecture is alluring. It is important to understand the disadvantages that could create problems during the transition to a full-time cloud infrastructure, including misconfiguration of cloud infrastructure architecture. Research reports details regarding the misconfiguration of Amazon S3 storage bucket have resulted in hackers retrieving 60,000 patient records. [17] Another cloud vulnerability exists in the firewall rules. This includes outbound access, access to non-HTTPS/HTTP ports, and inbound access on uncommon ports. Having knowledge of these issues early in the development stage of the cloud computing installation can help decrease the number of cyber incidents that will occur and impact the system and the storage of data assets in the cloud.

Intermountain Health and other healthcare organizations need to understand what their options are when developing plans to upgrade from a legacy system to a cloud computing infrastructure, platform, or service. Having knowledge of the benefits and the advantages cloud delivers, enables healthcare organizations to stay ahead of their competitors, build trust in their clients, and manage the security of data assets. When Intermountain Health and other healthcare organizations align usage of cloud computing with the recommendations and guidelines of the National Institute of Standards and Technology, this supports effective installation of information exchange that increases security and reduces risk. Applying a risk management strategy that aligns with the recommendations and guidelines of NIST special publication series can help Intermountain Health and other healthcare organizations, increase innovation and decrease costs. Adhering with the policy and laws enforced and enacted by the United States federal government, as well as state laws that services and business are conducted in, will help Intermountain Health and other healthcare organizations, increase efficiency of business operations, improve customer satisfaction, and decrease potential vulnerabilities within cloud computing information systems.

2.4 Effective Strategies for Healthcare Organization Cybersecurity Leadership

One of the most effective strategies to be applied to cybersecurity leadership as it aligns with healthcare organizations, is vendor management and relationship building. After all, it is simple to create methodologies to build alliances with third-party service and product providers for intimate business and government purposes, including sharing and storing sensitive data assets in information systems, hosted by third-party service providers. It is also important to establish the hierarchy of trust that should be established and designate who will be responsible for assessing those held accountable. Healthcare organizations relying on Amazon Web Services for information data asset storage and usage, as well as to increase security of information assets also must concern themselves with service level agreements (SLA), and the fine print enveloped in these agreements, to ensure liabilities by consumers are limited, and to ensure the CIA triad is not violated.

Therefore, one of the most important leadership roles today is the chief information officer (CIO). One of the most important leadership roles today is Chief Information Officer (CIO). This role is the co-anchor to the CEO and over sees the architect of business technology integration and IT management. The CIO enables an enterprise to reach its goals of success with technology and business software solutions. Without an effective CIO enabling better deployment of strategic planning methodologies, the enterprise can limit its own success. The role of CIO is instrumental in helping the enterprise assess its technology needs and determine how to align their goals with technology. This also enables the enterprise to better organize its databases and acquire the business software tools required to achieve short- and long-term goals. Research explains that daily responsibilities and requirements of a CIO are not what they once were, regardless, if someone is already in the position or aspiring to become a CIO. The CIO role is constantly evolving. Therefore, it is challenging to hire the right person to meet the demands of this role, and who understands the value of possessing the skills and expertise to conduct their responsibilities in alignment with the needs of each healthcare organization. [18]

In fact, the CIO should understand the value of communication and practice effective communication. Possessing effective communication skills enables the CIO to convey what is needed for the enterprise to achieve its goals and to effectively execute leadership. This includes understanding how to express technology language universally, so executive leaders can better assess how to allocate funding to invest in technology applications, i.e., software and hardware. Furthermore, it is important that the CIO embody the ability to think outside the box. This is important because each healthcare organization requires unique technology tools and management; making it imperatively important, the CIO is adaptive and capable of speaking professionally. The CIO must deploy strategies in alignment with the needs of the organization. The CIO must take the initiative to remain current in trends of technology and be able to share their modern technology architecture and landscaping ideals with the healthcare organization's stakeholders and IT leaders. Doing so enables personnel, stakeholders, as well as business and IT leaders to gain clarity of their roles and responsibility, to deploy all their efforts in alignment with the steps provided by the CIO, and to achieve the goals of the healthcare organization. It is also important that the CIO understand what the focus is of the healthcare organization's information development, data sharing, data storing, and data securing. CIOs are also required to be visionary leaders. [19]

2.4.1 Building vendor relationship trust

CIOs also must manage the relationship between vendors. To help convey the significance of vendor management, included are PowerPoint slides made into ping images to provide knowledge of this subject.

Establish vendor trust

Establishing vendor trust can be a daunting task; particularly, when relying on a team that is not trained to establish such relationships. When the IT manager and IT staff lack communication and organizational skills, it impacts the life cycle of the relationship.

Vendor assessment that works

Understanding the role of influence correlating to formal and psychological contracts in relationships with projects is critical to determining how to assess the appropriate vendor to meet the needs of a healthcare organization. Thus, to achieve this objective, it is imperative to comprehend four primary threats to project performance.

Threat one

Often, executive stakeholders and boards of directors lack the knowledge to determine what technology tools and applications are needed to operate business effectively. IT managers and IT staff must have the communication skills to educate these leaders to stipulate the value of technology integration in the workplace. Limiting the exchange of knowledge regarding technology integration, will impact how these leaders support the usage of new technology integration, as well as understand how to effectively utilize the technology.

Threat two

Vendors are external partners. Thus, IT managers and IT staff must research the services vendors offer to ensure they are receiving the services leased or purchased. Neglecting to do so, will increase threats to the organization information assets.

Threat three

Neglecting to read and understand the Service Level Agreement (SLA) will impact cost of service usage in the long-run. Third-party contracts for technology services require IT managers and IT staff to understand what is required to manage the vendor relationship for the life cycle of the contract. Lacking the knowledge of the SLA can impact the ability of the healthcare organization to terminate the agreement, if necessary.

Threat four

Ineffective vendor quality of services and products will impact the healthcare organization's ability to deploy effective technology management. This impedes the ability to develop a trustworthy business partnership. IT managers and IT staff working with vendors must assess the quality of services and products leased or purchased or suffer the consequences for neglecting to do so.

Vendor management lifecycle

- Increase vendor relationship with effective communication-verbally and written.
- Understand the contract and know the role and responsibilities of the vendor.
- Monitor all processes to ensure alignment with the organization's requirements.
- Define a clearly conveyed procurement strategy.
- Make necessary updates as needed to database data assets.
- Maintain written and digital records of all communication with vendors.

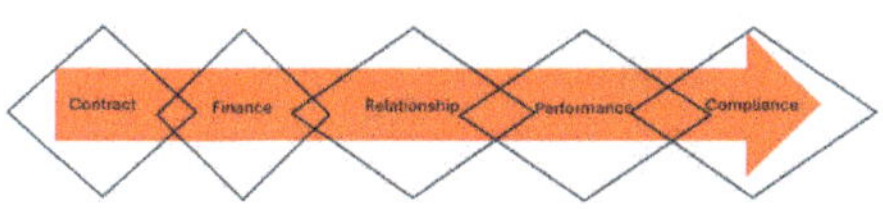

Aligning with COBIT 5

Governance is vital to vendor management. Governance must include risk optimization, resource optimization, and stakeholder transparency. Governance also should include:

- Aligning, planning, and organizing IT departments roles and responsibilities.
- Building, acquiring, and implementing.
- Delivering quality services and support.
- Monitoring, evaluating, assessing, and managing.

COBIT 5 organizational enablers

- Principles, policies, and frameworks
- Processes
- Organizational structures
- Culture, ethics, and behavior
- Information
- Services, infrastructures, and applications
- People, skills, and competencies

Clarity regarding roles and responsibilities of each executive leader when developing partnerships with vendors is essential to building strong bonds of support needed for healthcare organizations technology integration. Knowing how to communicate, verbally and in writing, reduces miscommunication and can prevent project management bloopers. Using COBIT 5 principles is a benefit healthcare organizations, IT managers must consider utilizing.

Building trust with vendors is a key part of vendor management. Maintaining written records of all documents, digitized or not, is a part of system back-up requirements. Working in alignment with COBIT 5 can be a key enabler of effective management efficiency. Having policies and providing training is key for successful vendor management.

2.5 Team Management

Team management is an essential element to effectively implement strategic planning within healthcare organizations. In fact, research compiled from Lawrence Miller explains that team management is a strategic methodology, encompassing all employees and personnel within a healthcare organization, who are instrumental in creating a high-performance culture. Team management is a system of managing performance through the total engagement of every employee and personnel working toward the aligned, measurable, performance goals and objectives of the healthcare organization. [20] Thus, the following PowerPoint presentation images deliver research regarding team management and its role in healthcare organizations' ability to effectively manage usage of technology tools and applications in the workplace.

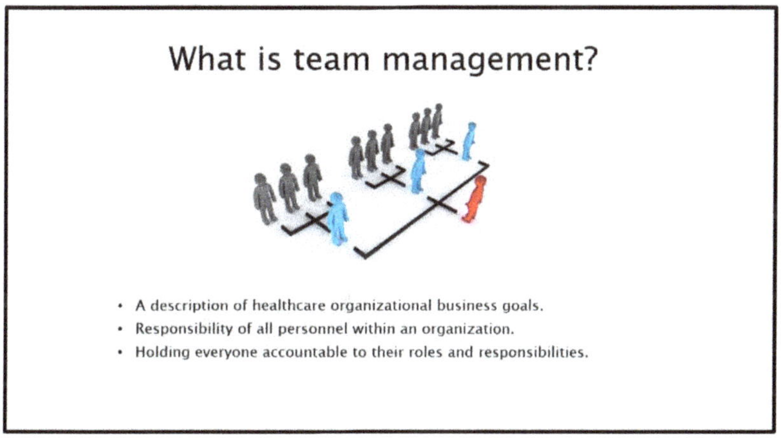

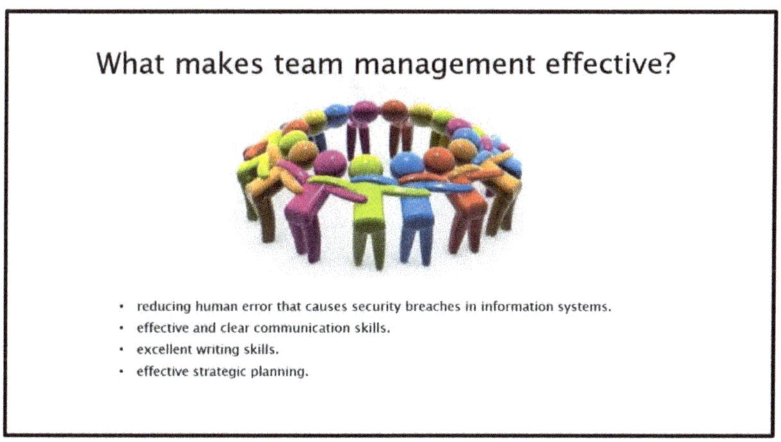

When is team management ineffective?
TEAM
❖ when clarity is absent regarding the role and responsibilities of each team contributor.
❖ when there is ineffective project management.
❖ when there is inappropriate neglect of policy compliance.
❖ when accountability for human error is absent and not penalized.

How to define team management?
• compiling lists of ideas and collecting feedback from the team.
• setting clear goals and objectives.
• setting a timeline for goals and objectives completion.
• ensuring everyone knows their role and responsibilities.
• staying humble.
• respecting everyone's input.

7 effective management skills
1. Clear and effective communication
2. Emotional intelligence
3. Organization
4. Ability to effective delegate responsibility
5. Openness
6. Problem-solving skills
7. Good decision-making skills

Thus, team management is an effective method to bridge the gap of communication between upper-, middle-, and low-level management and personnel. To be effective in team management requires the ability to listen to the ideas of each team member and write down the positive feedback provided from those team members, which can help the team achieve their overall goals and objectives. When there is a lack of communication, team members can become misguided and lose focus on their roles and responsibilities. Some essential steps to positive team management, include emotional intelligence, organization, the ability to delegate responsibilities, and solve problems effectively. This is an advantage that helps healthcare organizations achieve long- and short-term goals. The disadvantage of ineffective team management can result in monetary loss in the millions and/or damage to the healthcare organization's reputation. Therefore, effective team management should be strategically developed, implemented, and managed throughout the life cycle of the healthcare organization.

2.6 Summary

The central phenomenon engulfing cyberattacks deployed against healthcare organizations, globally, continues mounting monetary cost exceeding six-figure millions. This cost is a burden that healthcare organizations carry, which is leading to increased cost for consumers. The impact of ransomware attacks in the United States targeting healthcare organizations has reached an estimated $700 million. Globally, the cost is unknown. Legislation in the United States and around the world actively enact laws and modify older laws, to emphasis deterrence as a method of controlling these malicious acts of cyberattack. Still, these laws are not enough to make an alarming impact on decreasing the drive cybercriminals embody to feed on the known vulnerabilities woven in software and hardware applications utilized for healthcare organization's information systems. Having clarity on the problem enables healthcare organizations to make increased efforts to implement effective strategies to curve the growth of cyberattacks. One of the most invaluable strategies deployed is hiring skilled and knowledgeable information systems and information technology practitioners, who understand the significance of aligning usage and practice of technology tools, with the recommendations and guidelines enacted by industry regulations and standards. Most importantly, these professionals diligently align actions and methodologies with the enacted laws and policies authored by the U.S. Department of Defense that continues providing recommended methods of deterrence for both public and private sector. The National Security Agency (NSA) is instrumental in establishing baseline requirements for enhancing the skills and educational standards for institutions of higher education, by designating U.S. education institutions as centers of academic excellence and partnering with these institutions to prepare future cyber defense agents, to play a pivotal role in leading and managing information systems and information technology departments in public and private sector entities. The NSA is also invaluable with enforcing alignment of all workplace cybersecurity policy, information system policy, information technology policy, and cloud computing policy, with the recommended guidelines enacted and published by the U.S. Department of Commerce and its National Institute of Standards and Technology. Furthermore, efforts of the European Union have erected the General Data Protection Regulation (GDPR) in 2016, introducing a globalized standard of regulation that enforces the required privacy controls aligning with the United States legislation, on protecting consumer privacy and information assets. This is important because consumer healthcare information is sensitive and can lead to public embarrassment if released in the wrong hands.

However, these efforts alone are not enough to instill the level of fear required to stop cybercriminals from victimizing healthcare organizations and exploiting the known vulnerabilities integrated in their software and hardware applications. Thus, the effort to control risk associated with usage of these needed applications for storage of information assets, as well as for developing new documentation, continues facing an uphill battle. This battle can be won when healthcare organizations implement improved control risk management strategies that are uniquely defined by the workplace activities and personnel infrastructure, and technology needs and usage impacting the business operations and communication needs of each individual healthcare entity. There is no one-size-fits-all method to controlling the risk enveloped in software and hardware applications. No two healthcare organizations have the same services or products. No two healthcare organizations utilize the same technology tools, software, hardware, or possess the same data storage capacity needs. Therefore, each unique healthcare organization must introduce strategies that fit their own criteria.

One way to define a unique application of security is implementing cloud computing architecture applications. As mentioned in this chapter, Amazon Web Services has developed a dynamic and useful elastic healthcare record system that can be hosted in the cloud and can help deter external attacks from external threats. When encryption is applied to cloud computing, the onset of attack is limited because access to these application gateways is controlled by multi-factor authentication login access codes that should be only known by the cloud computing architect. When any entity is reliant on cloud computing architecture hosted by AWS, the level of support rendered by the service and product provider is defined by the usage of services, infrastructure, or platform. For instance, if utilizing AWS Software as a Service (SaaS), responsibility for managing and securing the application is rendered by the vendor. When using Infrastructure as a Service (IaaS), this requires end-users to define these applications themselves, including deployment, maintenance, and supporting, while AWS provides physical infrastructure. When using Platform as a Service (PaaS), AWS takes full control of deployment, maintenance, and supporting services.

However, unless the selected information system and information technology practitioners managing these environments are knowledgeable of the service level agreement (SLA) rendered by AWS and are aware of the responsibilities they are invested with, the level of security can be mismanaged and can lead to vulnerabilities being exploited. Thus, healthcare organizations need to continue increasing their knowledge of the role information systems and information technology plays in supporting their business communication and reliance of technology as a key conductor of daily operation. Executive leaders responsible for determining who has control over the planning and implementation of technology applications, must also stay knowledgeable and in tune with the trends in technology integration for healthcare organizations. Otherwise, the threat of cyberattack will persist.

Furthermore, cybersecurity leadership must play a pivotal role in helping increase knowledge sharing internally. Unless these selected leaders remain consistent with recommendations and guidelines enacted to support healthcare organizations, and their usage of technology tools and applications, the fault of cyber incidents falls in their laps. This level of human error impacts the reputation of any healthcare organization. Therefore, it is essential that healthcare organizations invest in providing their cybersecurity leaders and IT teams the continued educational support needed to stay ahead of the competition and competitors. Otherwise, the efforts implemented to deter successful cyberattacks will be useless.

2.7 Investigative Scenario

Botwest Memorial Hospital is in Sydney Paradigm, a major city in Pluto. This healthcare organization offers services to a diverse population of male and female, including pediatric services, cancer care and treatment, mental health services, surgical procedures, outpatient care, women's healthcare, and men's healthcare. They operate with a team of 13,000 employees, across

600 miles, through neighborhood clinics and the main hospital, as well as 24-hour emergency care location. Botwest Memorial Hospital relies on a third-party technology service and product provider that oversees their daily business usage and communication through the computer systems integrated throughout their healthcare organization. Utilizing a wide access network (WAN), local access network (LAN), as well as a local Internet service provider, Botwest Memorial Hospital remains open to vulnerability exploitation. The current staff of IT practitioners include one cybersecurity manager, who also plays the role of IT manager, and his team of 10 IT practitioners, are responsible for controlling the management of the current operating system relied on for business communication and data storage and development. The responsibilities include keeping the software in computers updated as recommended by the manufacturer, and updating security controls, i.e., firewalls and encryption. Of the 10 IT practitioners, five practitioners have bachelor's degrees in computer science. The cybersecurity and IT manager holds a CISSP, CISM, Bachelor of Science in Computer Science, and a graduate certificate in cybersecurity management. The other five IT practitioners have an associate degree in computer science as well as industry certificates in C++, network administration, and security+. The advancement of security controls is limited to the knowledge these practitioners possess as a collective body of knowledge. The cybersecurity and IT manager has not had training outside of the workplace in three years. The operating system relied on has not been updated as required by the manufacturer in two years.

What are some of the current threats to this workplace environment's usage of technology? How can external forces weave into the vulnerabilities engulfed in the current operating system? Who should be responsible for encouraging the cybersecurity and IT manager to attain current knowledge and training outside the workplace? What impact would a cyberattack have on Botwest Memorial Hospital? These are some of the issues and concerns enveloping healthcare organizations. Unless there are effective methods to control the risk of technology usage and reliance on such, Botwest Memorial Hospital and its consumers will be victimized. What must be done to correct this known vulnerability within this entity?

2.8 Discussion Questions

1. Why are cyberattacks growing against healthcare organizations?
2. What impact does human error play in EHR systems?
3. What benefit does usage of robotic processes envelop in automation?

4. How does executive leaders lack of knowledge regarding usage of legacy systems impact healthcare organizations?
5. In 2013, how much did Intermountain Healthcare operating income fall?
6. In 2023, what was the estimated number of people victimized by cyberattack deployed against their healthcare organization?
7. What year was the General Data Protection Regulation enacted?
8. What is HITRUST?
9. What is NIST 800-146 designed for?
10. What is NIST 800-53 Rev. 5 designed for?
11. What does the CIA triad represent?
12. What does COBIT 5 enable?

Glossary

Artificial intelligence – the simulation of intelligence humans possess and process through machines, including computer systems.

Bugs – a coding error in a programming script in software.

CIA triad – standard ethic of confidentiality, integrity, and availability of access to web-based interface, three pillars of information security.

CISM – certified information security manager.

CISSP – certified information systems security professional.

Dark web – web interface used to share information, links, data assets, and sensitive information not commonly transmitted and posted on the Internet, accessible through the Tor browser.

Elastic block store – an easy to utilize, scalable, high-performance block storage application developed for Amazon Elastic Computer Cloud (EC2) instances.

Elastic compute cloud – supports on-demand, scalable computing in AWS cloud.

Elastic container service – manageable container orchestration application service that supports simple deployment, management, and scalability of containerized applications.

Elastic disaster recovery – reduces downtime and loss of data, using swift recovery of on-premises and cloud-based applications utilizing affordable storage, minimal compute, and point-in-time recovery.

Elastic file system – renders serverless, full elastic file storage to support file sharing absent provisioning or managing storage capacity and performance output. Designed to scale on demand minus disrupting applications, increasing and reducing automatically when files are added or deleted.

HTTPS ports – hypertext transport protocol security ports that encrypt data as it is transferred across the Internet to communication endpoints.

Interface engines – utilized in healthcare organizations as an import endpoint to receive operations, and export endpoint for sending operations, and a way for transferring healthcare data via transmission control protocol and internet protocol communication (TCP/IP) between two endpoints.

Infrastructure as a Service – a concept of cloud computing the renders fundamental compute, network, and storage resources to consumers when they demand it, across the Internet, on a pay-as-you-go system. This enables end users to scale and reduce the cloud resources they utilize on a needed basis, and reduces reliability on high, up-front capital cost and unnecessary purchased infrastructure, particularly in the case of increased workloads.

Interoperability – the scale of software systems, devices, and applications configured and usable to transmit data assets across geographical locations to support healthcare organizations.

IP address – Internet protocol address that enables communication between devices and servers to transmit data through software and computer programming systems.

LAN – local access network used to connect to a Wi-Fi for Internet access in a home, office, or public location within a certain mile radius.

Load balancing – strategy to distribute network traffic equally across groups of resources that support software applications.

Service level agreement – a license agreement for services or products shared between a service or product provider and a consumer.

S3 storage bucket – storage service rendered by Amazon Web Services for leading scalability, data availability, security, and performance.

Software development life cycle – a consistent systematic way of organizing cost-effective and time-effective methods for developing and delivering quality software for the duration of the software usage.

Use cases – unique concepts of a system of devices, software, and applications that provide methods of usage.

WAN – wide area network delivers a broad scale of computer system connectivity through Wi-Fi and Internet from different geographical areas.

References

[1] Wager, A.K., Lee, W. F., & Glaser, P.J. (2022). Health Care Information Systems (5th Ed). Jossy Bass, John Wiley & Sons, Inc. Hoboken, N.J., p. 331

[2] Health Tech Digital, (2023, August 10). The Hidden Business Cost of Outdated Technology. [Website] Retrieved from: https://www.healthtechdigital.com/the-hidden-business-costs-of-outdated-technology/

[3] Davenport, T. & Kalakota, R. (2019). Digital Technology The potential for artificial intelligence in health care. [PDF] Retrieved from: https://www.ncbi.nlm.nih.gov/pmc/articles/PMC6616181/pdf/futurehealth-6-2-94.pdf

[4] Amazon Web Services, (2023). Electronic health record solutions in AWS Marketplace. [Website] Retrieved from: https://aws.amazon.com/marketplace/solutions/healthcare/health-records?aws-marketplace-cards.sort-by=item.additionalFields.headline&aws-marketplace-cards.sort-order=desc&awsf.aws-marketplace-healthcare-store-use-cases=*all

[5] Muoio, D. (2023, May 22). Intermountain Health logs 2.6% operating margin, $549M net income in Q1 2023. [Website] https://www.fiercehealthcare.com/providers/intermountain-health-logs-26-operating-margin-549m-net-income-q1-2023

[6] Southwick, R. (2023, December 18). Healthcare cyberattacks have affected more than 100 million people in 2023. [Website] Retrieved from: https://www.chiefhealthcareexecutive.com/view/health-data-cyberattacks-have-affected-more-than-100-million-people-in-2023

[7] Atler, S. (2023, November 17). October 2023 Healthcare Data Breach Report. [Website] Retrieved from: https://www.hipaajournal.com/october-2023-healthcare-data-breach-report/

[8] Muoio, D. (2022, April 6). Nonprofit systems Intermountain Health Care, SCL Health close 33-hospital merger. [Website] Retrieved from: https://www.fiercehealthcare.com/providers/intermountain-healthcare-scl-health-close-33-hospital-merger

[9] GuideStar, (n.d.). Intermountain Health Care, Inc. [Website] Retrieved from: https://www.guidestar.org/profile/74-2675605

[10] Common Exposures and Vulnerabilities, (2023). Search Results. [Website] https://cve.mitre.org/cgi-bin/cvekey.cgi?keyword=Intermountain+health

[11] Hegyi, M. (2023, June 15). HER in the Cloud: the elastic health record. [Website] Retrieved from: https://aws.amazon.com/blogs/publicsector/ehr-cloud-elastic-health-record/

[12] Al-Issa, Y., Ottom, A.M., Tamrawi, A. (2019, September 3). eHealth Cloud Security Challenges: A Survey. [Website] Retrieved from: https://www.ncbi.nlm.nih.gov/pmc/articles/PMC6745146/

[13] Amazon Web Services, (2023). What Is SDLC (Software Development Lifecycle)? [Website] Retrieved from: https://aws.amazon.com/what-is/sdlc/

[14] National Institute of Standards and Technology, (2012, May). Cloud Computing Synopsis and Recommendations. [PDF] Retrieved from: https://nvlpubs.nist.gov/nistpubs/Legacy/SP/nistspecialpublication800-146.pdf

[15] National Institute of Standards and Technology, (2014). Managing Risk in the Cloud. [PDF] Retrieved from: https://tsapps.nist.gov/publication/get_pdf.cfm?pub_id=919234

[16] National Institute of Standards and Technology, (2021). Managing the Security of Information Exchange. [PDF] Retrieved from: https://nvlpubs.nist.gov/nistpubs/SpecialPublications/NIST.SP.800-47r1.pdf

[17] Department of Health and Human Services, (2021). Threats in Healthcare Cloud Computing. [PDF] Retrieved from: https://www.hhs.gov/sites/default/files/threats-in-healthcare-cloud-computing.pdf

[18] Daniels, A. (2021, March 20). Information Week IT Network. Retrieved from: https://www.informationweek.com/strategic-cio/6-tips-for-it-pros-aspiring-to-be-a-modern-day-cio-/a/d-id/1340395

[19] Ghawe, S. A. & Brohman, K. (2016, March 20). CIO Leadership Characteristics and Styles. Retrieved from: https://core.ac.uk/download/pdf/301368883.pdf

[20] Miller, L. (2011, April 3). Team Management: The Core Practice of a High-Performance Organization. Retrieved from: https://www.lmmiller.com/wp-content/uploads/2011/06/Team-Management.pdf

3

Cybersecurity Leadership for Institutions of Higher Education

Learning Objectives

- Distinguish cybersecurity leadership for higher education.
- Examine current trends in higher education cyberattacks.
- Assess and develop effective planning and policy implementation.
- Assess artificial intelligence third-party service and products for higher education.

3.1 Introduction

Institutions of higher education have become targets for cyberattack. This growing central phenomenon is seemingly endless, impacting the ability to define a one-step method to deter these malicious attacks. Research reports staggering numbers of successful cyberattack incidents targeting higher education institutions, also convey the turnaround time for recovery after victimization is often three to four days. This timeline is further impacted by the inability of many higher education institutions to redefine plans of mitigation to effectively prepare for another cyberattack. The targeted asset typically includes accessing sensitive personal information of administrators, faculty, staff, and students as well as curriculum development architect, intellectual property, and research. The value of these assets continues growing, making higher education a prime target for cybercriminals. The United States executive branch has enacted new policy and passed new laws to deter increased cyberattacks. The European Commission mandated the General Data Protection Regulation (GDPR) to strategize an improved model of defeating and reducing the continued number of successful cyber incidents from escalating. This chapter provides a glimpse into the terrifying reality of cyberattacks being deployed against institutions of higher education around the globe. Each cyberattack incident differs greatly from another. However, there are shared similarities in how these institutions are being targeted. Thus, there is a need for improved investigation into these incidents to understand how to improve policy and training in institutions of higher education, to improve policy compliance among executive leaders, administrators, faculty, staff, and students, who are responsible for human error activities. Human error activities tend to be the primary gateway for cyberattack incidents to occur. Thus, this chapter enables you to learn how to assess cybersecurity leadership for higher education and develop effective planning strategies to implement improved cybersecurity leadership policy. Additionally, this chapter enables you to articulate artificial intelligence service and product provider, Amazon Web Services that delivers AI specifically for higher education, particularly, to increase deterrence of cyberattack. Finally, this chapter provides a summary of the facts and an investigative study, as well as discussion questions to reiterate your learning experience.

In an article titled *Higher Ed Is a Top Target for Cyber Criminals*, published by Bank of America in 2023, it was reported that a 157-year-old private college closed its doors permanently after being targeted with a ransomware attack. [1] Illinois-based private institution Lincoln College was victimized by a ransomware attack that cost this institution its reputation. Since 1865, this private liberal arts institution grew to become known as a predominately black institution, offering students grants and financial aid packages. The college began experiencing trouble during the COVID-19 pandemic and was forced to integrate technology as a medium to support learners' continued education. This began impacting student enrollment. After they were targeted by a ransomware attack, which the attackers demanded an estimated pay out of less than $100,000 to unleash the files being held captive, the institution was forced to close its doors. Sadly, this cyber incident is just a brief synopsis of what is occurring globally with institutions of higher ed. This phenomenon is costing institutions of higher education burdensome amounts of money and impacting their reputations, for not having effective cybersecurity leadership to control the risk aligned with their information systems and technology.

In 2022, the Black Cat ransomware gang successfully targeted North Carolina A & T State University, considered one of the largest black universities in America. This attack disrupted students' access to apps and systems utilized for instruction delivery and operation, including wireless learning management systems for online courses and single sign-on websites. [2] The Black Cat gang also claimed fame for the successful cyberattack that targeted Florida International University, where 1.2 terabytes of data were confiscated. Additional institutions of higher education targeted by ransomware attacks in 2022, include University of Detroit Mercy, Centralia

College, Phillips Community College of the University of Arkansas, National University College, and Savannah State University. This merely denotes a peak of ransomware cyberattack incidents, institutions of higher education experienced.

In fact, additional research collected from abroad conveys that in 2017, MacEwan University in Edmonton, Canada was victimized by a cyberattack, due to a human error incident deployed by a staff member, who fell prey to a phishing attack that cost the university $11.8 million. [3] Reports explain that the staff member opened an email that requested banking details, which the staff member assumed the bank logo and information was valid. Had the Canadian Shared Security Operations Centre (CanSSOC) not been established back in 2021, institutions of higher education would not be allowed to share information about cybersecurity attacks, they had or were experiencing, with the public. Research explains that since this organization advocated for this change, there has been improved sharing of resources and information regarding cyberattacks, successfully targeting institutions of higher education in the UK and Australia. [4] The goal of this initiative is to enable Canadian institutions to gain access to information and details about known successful cyberattack incidents that have occurred, as well as gain clarity on potential threats and security breaches.

Another university that experienced a ransomware attack costing £450,000, was University of the West of Scotland. A ransomware gang known as Rhysida, exploited the university's network vulnerabilities and gained access to sensitive data files belonging to staff and students. The university's staff laptops were infiltrated, much of the university's IT systems were shut down, and students were not able to submit assignments. [5] As a result of this attack, staff's banking information was disseminated on the dark web as well as national insurance numbers and sensitive university documents. However, ransomware attacks are not the only method of cyberattack universities are experiencing.

In May 2021, many Belgium universities were targeted successfully with distributed denial of service attacks (DDOSAs), which initially targeted the country's government agencies. This attack method prevented university students from accessing online courses and logging into their university research databases. [6] In 2022, the University of Neuchâtel was successfully targeted due to a known vulnerability in the Microsoft Exchange Server used for email accounts and calendars, that enabled cybercriminals to insert encryption trojans. Although the National Cyber Security Centre alerted over 4500 businesses and local authorities about this issue a year prior to this incident, mitigation efforts remained slow, resulting in continued successful exploitation. [7] One year later, in February 2023, the University of Zurich was successfully victimized with a cyberattack. Research explains higher ed institutions in Germany and Austria have been experiencing increased cyberattack incidents, which resulted in university's IT systems being shut down for days. [8]

Additional research reports that a dangerous organization known as TA453 deployed a sophisticated cyberattack using social engineering techniques to access public intellectuals in the Middle East, including university professors and members of think tanks. [9] This attack involved masking invitations to a debate regarding SOAS London University, a leading institution of higher education, who specializes in Asia, Africa, and Middle Eastern studies. It is believed that the goal of this scheme was to collect sensitive information for the Islamic Revolutionary Guard Corps, which is listed as a terrorist group with the United States federal authorities. Victims were discovered using an algorithm that relied on artificial generative intelligence to compile a list of known scholars with knowledge of the Middle Eastern academic world. A phishing attack link was used to lure victims to the designated website, where victims shared sensitive details identifying them and their credentials correlating with universities.

This growing phenomenon is crippling many institutions who lack efficient resources and information system and technology practitioners, who understand how to manage technology tools, applications, software, and hardware. When paired with ineffective strategies of effective development and implementation of training administrators, faculty, staff, and students about cyberattack methods and models being deployed, it is difficult to discern best practices to be applied across all universities and colleges. There are organizations being established in different countries to tackle this issue and partner with government agencies. The continued relaxed state of mind toward the potential risks of a successful cyberattack many universities and colleges are exhibiting, can be detrimental to the safety of faculty and students as well as the reputation of these institutions. Having some leverage of control over the technology tools and applications relied on is not enough. The sophisticated methods and strategies being implemented by cybercriminals is escalating annually, as it has become a known fact that institutions of higher education are easy prey for successful cyberattack incidents and possible payloads. However, there is always a way to deter successful attacks from occurring when knowledge sharing is a method in preparing a reliable cyber defense. Knowing how to assess cybersecurity leadership for higher education and develop effective planning strategies to implement improved cybersecurity leadership and deterrence, are first steps in combating these unauthorized intrusions into sensitive information files. One method I found interesting in helping colleges and universities achieve improved cybersecurity leadership was introduced in Croatia. The research article titled *Advanced Digital Maturity in Croatia's Higher Education System* discusses a plethora of resources that outline effective ways of assessing, developing, implementing, and managing cyberattack risk targeting higher ed.

One of the most ignored methods of deterrence in institutions of higher education is effective assessment of cybersecurity leadership and effective planning and development of strategies that improve cybersecurity leadership and deterrence. Research compiled from the European Union, which authored and published a research study titled *Advancing Digital Maturity in Croatia's Higher Education System*, in April 2023, proposed three structured frameworks for improving cybersecurity leadership in institutions of higher education, including digital leadership, digital infrastructure, and digital competence and culture. [10] Digital leadership is evident when institutions of higher education possess a comprehensive and strategic outlook for technology integration at all scales of the institution's needs and capacity, to effectively implement technology as a key component to managing and delivering services and products. This aligns with the CIA triad – confidentiality, integrity, and availability. This includes alignment of all institution activities and processes that correlate with business operations and communication, through all technology infrastructures relied on. Digital infrastructure means institutions of higher education possess knowledge and embody intelligence to effectively access, connect, and utilize all technology, including physical equipment, software, and technical support services rendered by third-party service and product providers, needed to enable daily operation of business and communication across the institution to benefit from the integration of the digital conversion. Digital competence and culture means institutions of higher education effectively manage internal policies. It also means aligning all daily business operations and communication practice to meet the objectives of the policies to support the cultivation of the unique skills, intelligence, and knowledge of all individuals that help manage the institution, i.e., executive leaders, academic staff and faculty, and students. This also includes effectively and successfully engaging with the technology tools, software, hardware, and applications required to operate an efficient place of business in alignment with federal laws and regulations, domestically and internationally, and reducing human error.

Using this approach but modifying to meet the needs of any institution of higher education, can be instrumental in supporting the digital maturity governance and cybersecurity leadership needed for any institution of higher education. According to this proposed framework designed with institutions of higher education in Croatia in mind, and using quantitative and qualitative research methods, helps outline this strategy that should be adopted by institutions of higher education. Although the type of technology tools and assets relied on from one institution to another differs, the focus is defined by the three structured frameworks, i.e., digital leadership, digital infrastructure, and digital competence and culture. Using the e-learning schooling platform across 151 primary and secondary institutions in Croatia, it was proposed that infrastructure and emphasizes of adherence with the proposed infrastructure, would be helpful toward achieving the best outcome. In alignment with these objectives the common areas presented in Table 3.1 are key areas of infrastructure that require effective management and risk control management in institutions of higher education.

Digital maturity in institutions of higher education must incorporate effective planning management and leadership as essential components to control how technology tools are relied on and implemented for daily operation and communication. When these tools are mismanaged and training is limited, there is room for increased risks and increased cyber threats to manifest. When threats are not contained, they can result in vulnerabilities being exploited. Thus, it is imperative to plan effective deterrence methods, increase management training and hands-on experience, and implement leadership guidance that control risks across the institution. Planning for cyberattacks ahead of an actual attack is essential in preparing to defend against known attack methods that have been used to attack competitors' information systems and technology tools. The continued deployment of ransomware attacks proves this type of attack is prevalent and consistent. Other attack methods include phishing, social engineering, and human error. Therefore, using multiple methods of deterrence helps build a layer of security that is impenetrable. Using current applications of security is valuable to the development and implementation of this strategy. When ignored, any institution leaves itself open to victimization, not once but continually. Planning must embody knowing the method of attack, tools that are commonly used to deploy an attack, how to recover quickly from an attack if such is successful, and who to hold accountable within each department after the attack occurs. Thus, training becomes more vital toward controlling this risk. When training is developed correctly and implemented effectively, there are positive benefits that shield an institution against victimization. Any institution of higher education that neglects to train executive leaders about phishing attacks, social engineering attacks, email attacks, and whaling schemes, as well as exploitation methods, is neglecting to prepare and plan an effective strategy of deterrence.

Table 3.1 Common infrastructure areas in institutions of higher education.

Planning, management, and leadership	Teaching and learning with technology	Innovative digital maturity	Information systems and technology culture	Information systems and technology infrastructure
Planning effective deterrence methods, increasing management training and hands-on experience, and implementing leadership guidance that controls risk across the institution.	Determining the best method of introducing administrators, faculty, and staff to technology, both for face-to-face learning and asynchronous learning management systems.	Using current trends in information systems and technology training that can be updated as needed by executive leadership and administrators.	Limiting access to technology tools and information assets by executive leaders, administrators, faculty, and staff.	Making sure all relied on IST assets are currently configured correctly.
Determining methods of integration of information systems and technology.	Providing awareness training of all technology tools, software, and hardware relied on, and providing consistent training and assessment of such training.	Using recommended guidelines from the National Institute of Standards and Technology SP-800 series and modifying these recommendations to align with each institution's needs.	Limiting access to technology and information assets by students.	Creating a systematic hierarchy of responsibility that holds each person accountable for the actions of others.
Implementing clearly conveyed information and cybersecurity policy and compliance regulation and penalties for noncompliance.	Creating curriculum and instruction that cultivates end users' confidence in usage of these applications, tools, and systems.	Building confidence in those who are required to use technology daily for business operations and communication.	Managing clearly written reports that assess human error incidents before and after training, keeping record of all incidents, causes of all incidents, the responses deployed, and timeline of each incident discovered.	Ensuring the network is impenetrable, using baseline procedures for intrusion detection and intrusion prevention.
Introducing effective assessments and auditing that aligns with federal and state law and policy.	Creating policy controls that reduce risks and human error incidents.	Defining multiple layers of security that protect all end users from cyberattack victimization.	Deploying consistent drills that test the awareness skills of all end users at all levels, i.e., executive leaders, administrators, faculty, staff, and students.	Employing cryptology methods that secure information in transit and at rest.

Determining methods of integration of information systems and technology is vital to knowing what technology tools must be used daily and what is required to manage those technology tools effectively. Installing technology without securing that technology creates a threat to the entire infrastructure. Thus, it is important to know how to configure all technology tools for usage by laypersons. This means all information systems, information technology, and cloud (ISTC) practitioners are held accountable and responsible for making sure all technology tools are secured correctly. This means checking all remote access entrance points to ensure they are configured to prevent unauthorized access to these controls is a norm. This means ensuring each person is using their own technology devices and not accessing another's. This means enforcing how security is respected and assessed to ensure compliance is effective. Unless everyone works together, there is room for misinterpretation of responsibilities. There is also room for human error to become instrumental in creating a gateway for penetrating the system and technology tools.

Implementing clearly conveyed information security and cybersecurity policy and compliance regulation and penalties for noncompliance, is another step in establishing digital maturity. The fact that most institutions of higher education, domestically and internationally, receive a bulk of funding from government agencies, requires these institutions to align their information systems and technology tool usage with the laws mandated and enacted by the government, not just domestically but internationally. One way to achieve this alignment is integrating the recommendations from the National Institute of Standards and Technology Special Publication 800 series. Commonly relied on policy include 800-53 Revision 5 regarding security and privacy controls for information systems and organizations. This publication delivers essential guidelines for security and privacy engineering principles, security and privacy architect, enterprise architecture, auditing reviewing and reporting, boundary protection, wireless link protection, methods of denial-of-service protection, and methods of preventing unauthorized access to data and information in shared resources. Next is NIST 800-30 regarding information security. This helps ISTC practitioners effectively conduct audits within institutions of higher education for risks management. This policy was introduced by the Joint Task Force Transformation Initiative Interagency Working Group in alignment with representatives from the Civil, Defense, and Intelligence community. Delivered in correlation with support from the National Institute of Standards and Technology and senior leaders from the U.S. Department of Commerce and Defense, Office of the Director of National Intelligence, as well as the Committee on National Security Systems. [11] This publication outlines the risk management process, how to deploy a risk assessment, key risk concepts, applications of risk assessments, the process of preparing for a risk assessment, steps in conducting a risk assessment, how to communicate and who to share such communication with regarding risk assessment outcomes, and methods of maintaining a risk assessment during the life cycle. Using this guideline provides additional layers of security and helps minimize risk of applications, software, hardware, and technology tools used daily across the entire institution and various departments within institutions of higher education, administrative offices, department offices, research department offices, libraries, and faculty and staff departments and offices.

Furthermore, it is recommended to assess the recommendations and guidelines rendered by the Rand corporation, who published a dynamic research study supporting the need for increased knowledge engulfing cybersecurity policy. In the published guide titled *A Framework for Exploring Cybersecurity Policy Options*, Rand corporation expresses that the goal of this project was to create a framework for cybersecurity that joins government, industry, and academic institutions and to understand the significance of these key stakeholders in partnering with one another. [12] It is presented that usage of an overarching policy direction be the guide for governing how cybersecurity leadership plays a dynamic role of responsibilities across the entire institution of higher education. These roles focus on management regarding the who, what, when, where, and how. However, it is one thing to assess dynamics of management and another to effectively install value of management that is adhered and respected by all parties within the institution, to deploy a systematic method of controlling risk factors. Next are rights. In this case, it is believed that the usage of policy within institutions of higher education needs to align with the beliefs and culture of the institution and its executive leaders, administrators, faculty, staff, and students, who, too, must align their activities and actions in alignment with the culture and beliefs of the institution and its purpose for installing policy. This includes governance of cybersecurity policy. Without control of an institution's culture and belief ecosystem, the chance of deterrence being effective continues being reduced with each cyberattack incident.

Additionally, is roles and obligations, which often are ignored because too many times executive leaders and administrators are playing multiple roles and irresponsibly deploying actions and activities that often neglect to emphasize the value of cybersecurity and alignment with the policies enacted to control risk management. When government mandates policy controls and shares those with industry and academic institutions and the policy controls are ignored and ineffectively introduced, the fault falls on to the institutions of higher education, while the industry fails to alarm end users of continued vulnerabilities integrated in technology tools and applications. It is not until a catastrophic event occurs and it is broadcast globally that knowledge sharing begins. Next is governance, which is partnered between public and private sectors. When one fails to be effective, the other suffers. Finally, the incentive structure is reduced because too often incentives are not valued enough by end users.

Thus, keeping aligned with innovative concepts of assessing the role and regulations of governance and management of institutions of higher education, through systematic auditing, is an intelligent method of minimizing the ongoing imbalance of cybersecurity leadership. This means, introducing an auditing process that holds these institutions accountable under government laws, domestically and internationally. When considering the introduction of the State of New York NYDFS Cybersecurity Regulation (23 NYCRR 500), a new regulation that was introduced in February 2017, outlining standards and requirements for developing and implementing effective cybersecurity programming to control the seemingly endless number of sophisticated cyberattack incidents impacting financial institutions. This imposes strict methods of covering financial institutions, including enforcing the need for a chief information security officer, the enactment of comprehensive cybersecurity policy, and the initiation of ongoing reporting and auditing systems regarding cybersecurity events. It is coupled with reliance on NIST special publication recommendations and guidelines, including implementing new reporting requirements of all cyberattack incidents and imposing strict fines reaching $100,000, daily for violators. It creates an innovative way of enforcing compliance and adherence among institutions of higher education. However, to maintain optimal performance requires institutions of higher education to employ trained and qualified ISTC practitioners, who are knowledgeable of these mandated policies and who can effectively implement procedures of operation and auditing that protects the institution and trains end users effectively.

The next key component is teaching and learning with technology, which plays a role in how cybersecurity leadership aligns with institutions of higher education, specifically because the European Union emphasized this in its research report, conveying the value of determining the best method of introducing administrators, faculty, and staff to technology, both for face-to-face learning and asynchronous learning management systems, which is essential to controlling risk management. Without effective teaching and learning methods, institutions of higher education risk being undermined by competitors and place themselves in a low-ranking status of offering innovative concepts of education. After all, e-learning is an innovative concept that institutions of higher education utilize to build global student bodies and integrate their services and products into communities worldwide. When institutions of higher education establish their unique model of teaching and learning, they are reliant on secure learning management systems provided by third-party service and product providers. Thus, controlling risk associated with usage of learning management systems become an extended component of the digital maturity for institutions of higher education. To achieve enhanced cybersecurity leadership through third-party service providers, who deliver learning management system applications and tools, requires understanding service language agreements and knowing how these partnerships are aligned with delivery of services for institutions of higher education, in alignment with government laws and policy, domestically and internationally.

In addition, it is important to provide awareness training of all technology tools, software, and hardware relied on, and provide consistent training throughout the lifecycle and assess those completing such training. Training is essential to staying current with trends in cyberattack methods. Not only must ISTC practitioners stay current in trends, but executive leaders, administrators, faculty, staff, and students. Each of these groups need to be aware of how to utilize all technology tools and how to deploy their actions, roles, and responsibilities to help secure these tools effectively. Otherwise, there is the continued burden of implementing security strategies that seem meaningless.

The National Institute of Standards and Technology implemented the National Initiative of Cybersecurity Workforce framework in August 2017, as a way of encouraging workplace information systems and technology practitioner of aligning their efforts, roles, and responsibilities with governance and management concepts proven effective when implemented and aligned with recommendations and guidelines. Although the applications rendered differ from one institution of higher education to another, this framework remains a vital component to preparing workplace cybersecurity training. Thus, as outlined in this instructional guideline, published under NIST SP 800-181, this reference resource outlines guidance regarding cybersecurity work and knowledge, skills, and abilities required to secure each tasks deployed to improve cybersecurity posture within any organization. Therefore, institutions of higher education are great environments to integrate this concept of protection measure. In doing so, institutions of higher education add additional layers of security that can enhance the protective applications to deter successful cyberattacks against networks and information systems and technology.

As outlined, benefits of this framework include training infrastructure that focuses on specialty areas within the workplace, work roles, knowledge, skills, and abilities, as well as tasks. This tool also provides clarity regarding the identification of the cybersecurity workforce needs and requirements, conveys methods of recruitment and hiring of skillful cybersecurity talent, stages of education and training that cybersecurity workforce members should possess minimally, as well as offer retention and development of highly skilled cybersecurity talent. This framework delivers an identifiable reference for job titles as they relate to cybersecurity in the workplace.

For instance, there are clear task-related duties of operation that align with work roles. This includes conveying a description of the work role, what each role is expected to perform, what each work role is expected to exhibit, what each work role is expected to possess, and what each work role is expected to demonstrate. Work roles include authorizing official, security control assessor, software developer, secure software assessor, enterprise architect, security architect, research and development specialist, systems requirements planner, systems test and evaluator specialist, information systems security developer, systems developer, database administrator, data analyst, knowledge manager, technical support specialist, network operations specialist, systems administrator, systems security analyst, cyber legal advisor, privacy officer/privacy compliance manager, cyber instructional curriculum developer, cyber instructor, information systems security manager, communication security manager, cyber workforce developer and manager, cyber policy and strategy planner, executive cyber leadership, program manager, information technology project manager, product support manager, IT investment/portfolio manager, IT program auditor, cyber defense analyst, cyber defense infrastructure support specialist, cyber defense incident responder, vulnerability assessment analyst, threat warning/analyst, exploitation analyst, target network analyst, and cyber intel planner. [13] While these roles may not be present in all institutions of higher education, the ISTC practitioner tends to be responsible for multiple roles and required to deploy the responsibilities engulfed in these roles to effectively safeguard their workplace and the technology tools relied on. When these individuals fall short, cybersecurity leadership suffers greatly and hinders the ability for the institutions to effectively protect technology tools and applications from cyberattack victimization. Therefore, utilization of this framework should be a necessity that is never ignored. While the method may not be useful in all institutions of higher education, implementing as many as possible increases the chances of defeating the efforts of cyber threats.

Building confidence in those who are required to use technology daily for business operations and communication is also important. When end users lack confidence in using technology for business purposes, it can impact their ability to remain complaint with workplace cybersecurity policy and recommended actions and procedures. While training is essential, it is also important to assess those being trained as often as necessary to ensure everyone is capable of being a cyber defense vector in protecting the institution from cyberattack. Knowing how to open new documents in a Word application and save that document and secure that document with password protection is critical to ensuring security firewalls are being implemented and acknowledged. Knowing how to secure a file before sending it in an attachment across the institution's network via a public Wi-Fi into a secure network on a private Wi-Fi, is also important. Too often end users lack this knowledge and act without second thought of security measures. This human error creates a gateway for cyberattackers to gain entrance into a vulnerable system. Building confidence also enables end users to respect the purpose of security policy and conduct workplace business practices and procedures as required to reduce successful cyberattack incidents. When everyone does their part correctly, effectively, and securely, it provides a harmonious scale of security balance.

Defining multiple layers of security that protect all end users from cyberattack victimization is also important. When multiple layers of security are applied to any information system and technology tools and applications, there is a 99.99% chance the number of attacks will be reduced. Keeping current with multi-factor authentication recommendations is beneficial to adding a layer of security. However, there is no 100% preventative measure that stops cyberattacks from happening. In fact, research published by the National Library of Medicine National Center of Biotechnology Information in May 2013, under the title Secure Methods for Biometric-Based Recognition with Integrated Cryptographic Functions, this article explains that utilizing biometric authentication for security embodies threats. [14] Thus, it is essential to try and align all layers of security applications with recommended guidelines for securing technology tools. Since email communication is a vital asset in institutions of higher education, ISTC practitioners and executive leaders, administrators, faculty, staff, and students need to be aware of communication security.

Research explains that use of cable and wireless radio transmitted channels across different telecommunication environments, information categories, and data formats that align with information traveling across telecommunication applications and layers, is supported by packet-based internet protocol (IP) data networks. [15] However, additional data formats and transport mechanisms persist. In fact, mobile cellular networks, wireless local networks as well as traditional landline networks do not operate with other telecommunication infrastructure that work with different standards and formats at a lower scale of the operating system interface. Thus, the common usage of IP packets within a network layer enables standard techniques for securing data that is supposed to be secured because it is sensitive private information, i.e., executive leaders' home addresses, their mobile phone numbers, their bank routing numbers, and their personal medical information, as well as the same information belonging to administrators, faculty, staff, and students. When end users have knowledge of this reality and are trained to help protect these assets from unauthorized users, it provides an additional layer of confidence needed to manage their role and responsibilities daily, in alignment with cybersecurity policy. When there is an imbalance in compliance, it creates the gateway for threats to become vulnerabilities.

Another important component is information systems and technology culture. Limiting access to technology tools and information by executive leadership, administrators, faculty, staff, and students is crucial to maintain security over sensitive and vital information and technology tools. When there is a limitation on who has access to vital information resources that identify individual's personal information, there is greater opportunity to maintain security over that information. Research reported by the National Center for Education Statistics explains that restricting the handling of sensitive information to authorized personnel is important, and that appropriate clearance should only be given to those who have authorization to access that vital information. [16] In fact, as stated previously, due to the agreement shared between the U.S. Department of Education and public and private institutions of higher education that receive federal student aid grants and loans, as well as unsubsidized and subsidized funding, these institutions are held accountable for protecting their information systems from unauthorized users. The Federal Information Security Modernization Act (FISMA) outlines some of the regulations mandated for institutions of higher education to align their information systems security controls with. To be compliant with this Act requires conducting audits of the information security program to keep risk at an acceptable level. [17] However, although the Federal Information Security Modernization Act sets the legal requirements for annual compliance, authority has been bestowed to the National Institute of Standards and Technology (NIST), the government body responsible for creating standards and policies that institutions of higher education should be aligning with regarding security controls to ensure their systems, applications, and networks continue being secured. As previously mentioned, NIST policies correlating with this include NIST SP 800-53 – Security and Privacy Controls for Information Systems and Organization, NIST SP 800-35 – Guide to Information Technology Security Services, NIST SP 800-39 – Managing Information Security Risk: Organization, Mission, and Information System View, NIST SP 800-37, Revision 2, Risk Management Framework for Information Systems and Organizations: A system Life Cycle Approach for Security and Privacy, as well as others, including NIST CSWP 29 – Cybersecurity Framework 2.0.

Instilling strict regulations regarding usage of effective applications for security control should not just be targeted toward executive leadership, administrators, faculty, or staff. Students also play a role in helping protect institutions of higher education from cyberattack victimization. Usage of multifactor authentication login credentials is the best method of deploying additional layers of security control. However, too often these credentials, i.e., username and passwords are shared among students to access resources both on campus and off campus. Research explains that institutions of higher education should adopt passwordless multi-factor authentication solutions that control X.509 certificates or FID02 keys. [18] Research explains some benefits for using passwordless credentials, is reducing the stress for institution of higher education, IT staff from needing to constantly update password credentials. This also enforces protection against phishing emails and phishing attacks. It is also beneficial because it eliminates the need to continue creating new passwords and resetting passwords. It also helps avoid multi-factor authentication fatigue. Another benefit is that this helps institutions of higher education to remain compliant with requirements of the FISMA. This also provides protection from phishing and man-in-the-middle attacks.

Additionally important with information systems and technology culture, is managing clearly written reports that assess human error incidents before and after training, and regarding keeping records of all incidents, including what caused the incident, what the response of the incident was, and the timeline it took to discover the incident and to mitigate the incident. The National Institute of Standards and Technology created a policy that helps institutions of higher education effectively comply with this requirement. NIST SP 800-61, Rev. 2 Computer Security Incident Handling Guide, is one example of a policy that should be assessed to ensure alignment with compliance regulatory within institutions of higher education. [19] Keep in mind, since many institutions of higher education offer online degree and certificate programs to a global student body, these regulations are also applied to international engagement. In fact, the European Commission General Data Protection Regulation (GDPR) is the number one policy that must be adhered to, or these institutions of higher education will face civil liabilities and financial penalties imposed by the European Commission, but only if these institutions provide educational services to European students. Thus, to help institutions of higher education achieve greater control over potential risk factors with their information systems and technology infrastructure, the National Institute of Standards and Technology published the Cybersecurity Incident Response Plan in October 2023. [20] This is a detailed plan that provides sufficient clarity and details of instructions to support the needs of any organization in preparing for pre-cyberattack incidents and post-cyberattack mitigation. Utilizing the recommendations in this plan are key elements to support the risks factors aligned with cybersecurity incidents targeting institutions of higher education.

One of the most useful developments in preparing for cyberattacks in institutions of higher education is deploying consistent drills that test the awareness skills of all end users at all levels, i.e., executive leaders, administrators, faculty, and staff. Ensuring these key players are knowledgeable of cyberattack methods, i.e., email phishing, distributed denial of service attacks, Trojans, viruses, malware, ransomware, spear fishing, whaling, man-in-the-middle, brute force attacks, etc. As well as knowledgeable of how to contain an incident and report the incident clearly, is an important factor in training and preparing these key individuals. The U.S. Cybersecurity & Infrastructure Security Agency delivers online training that is useful in preparing institutions of higher education to improve their overall training for these key personnel. Training is offered in areas such as incident response training. [21] Utilizing this training provides awareness webinars, with topics including:

- Defending Internet accessible systems
- Preventing web and email server attacks
- Preventing DNS infrastructure tampering
- Introduction to network diagramming
- Understanding indicators of compromise
- Defense against ransomware attacks
- Log management
- Methods of using the CISA incident response playbook for your organization

Of course, additional training material is provided, including cyber range training and on-demand training, which provides a ransomware overview, detailing how to block malicious IP, how to sinkhole malicious domains, how to disable server message block, how to create application-allow-listing policies, and how to back up and restore Active Directories. There are also virtual online training recordings in video format delivered via the CISA YouTube channel.

The last vital area of focus is information systems and technology infrastructure. This is important because ensuring all relied on information systems and technology tools and assets are configured correctly, is key to ensure security is applied efficiently. Incorrectly configuring software and hardware is a leading cause of threats and vulnerabilities. The U.S. Department of Defense provides an open-source website interface that renders clarity and useful information regarding the value of configuring software and hardware applications to ensure increased security is applied to these tools and systems. When vulnerabilities result in cyberattacks, it enables cybercriminals to gain access to systems and retrieve data and deploy malicious attack activities, including malware and ransomware. Research reported in 2023 conveyed that configuration errors are commonly responsible for almost one-third of data breaches deployed in 2021, and it was anticipated to also cause 99% of all firewall breaches throughout 2023. [22] Furthermore, it was reported that misconfiguration security issues can also cause security gaps that expose applications to cyberattack risks. It is believed that system administrators tend to neglect to change the default configuration of devices or applications while conducting installations of these new systems, software, and applications, into an information systems and technology management console. This error creates the problem because it enables attackers to deploy automated attacks by testing if a targeted system is using a default setting. When default settings are reconfigured and new passwords are implemented, there is greater chance of preventing a successful cyberattack from occurring. Thus, training ISTC practitioners is more important than training end users, who, too, utilize the technology and information system of institutions of higher education. When ISTC practitioners short-change their responsibilities, the organization suffers greatly.

In fact, creating a systematic hierarchy of responsibility that holds each person accountable for the actions of others, is a first step in controlling risks factors that enable successful cyberattack incidents at institutions of higher education. This hierarchy starts with the president of the institution, who is vital in preparing and educating their administration in understanding the significance of effectively managing security of all information systems and technology. The next person in the hierarchy is the vice president, deans, provost, and emeritus. The training rendered to these top-level leaders should include knowledge training on the computer operating system relied on for daily usage, i.e., Windows operating systems and/or Linux. It is also important to understand that software applications differ from institution to institution. Thus, having effective partnerships with all software service providers that may have training deliverable via online platforms, is a dynamic way to provide these leaders the current trends in training, ISTC practitioners from needing to develop training that they are not trained to effectively provide. This is supportive in decreasing the chance of providing ineffective training models that do not meet the needs of institutions of higher education.

The next level of this hierarchy is faculty and staff. Rendering quality training regarding usage of approved software for teaching and learning, is vital to ensuring these applications are compatible with the current usage of software and hardware relied on. It is also important to ensure these applications are configured to provide some level of security throughout the lifecycle. If there is an issue of incompatibility, it is imperative to consider implementing a software application that can be easily aligned with the current system and that provides the scale of security needed to protect other applications from being targets of entrance points. It takes one or two vulnerabilities in the whole information system to enable cyberattackers to gain access to the system.

Furthermore, policy development and implementation, should be rendered through effective training with a focus on usage of information systems and technology, used in daily business and communication operations within institutions of higher education. Having control over the creation of useful policies is important to accountability measures being adhered to and respected. When policy is not developed and implemented correctly, it creates the gateway for human error to play a significant role in supporting cyberattacks to occur. As pointed out previously, research convey that human error remains a contributing factor to the increase in information systems attacks and data breaches at institutions of higher education. [23]

Another step in securing institutions of higher education against cyberattacks, is ensuring the network is impenetrable by using baseline procedures for intrusion detection and intrusion prevention. Today, there are many service providers who offer intrusion detection and intrusion prevention software. However, not all service and product providers provide quality services and products. Ineffective quality of services and products can lead to vulnerabilities being overlooked during the installation of an intrusion detection or intrusion prevention software application. For example, institutions of higher education are often targets for Distributed Denial of Service Attacks (DDoSA). Therefore, using an intrusion detection application can be instrumental in deterring a successful DDoSA. However, unless the service provider delivers a quality IDS, there is greater chance a cyberattacker can gain access to the network and impact the ability for traffic to access that network.

Amazon Web Service is one quality service and product provider that renders reliable and trusted IDS/IPS. Research reports that intrusion detection systems (IDS) monitor networks and/or systems searching for malicious activity and/or policy violations. IDS provide reports for the system administrator or a security information and event management system. [24] Intrusion prevention systems are located behind firewalls and deliver increased layers of security by scanning and analyzing unusual content that is a potential threat. When correctly configured this places the IPS in the communication path to deploy system alarms when suspicious traffic is discovered within a network.

Institutions of higher education can improve their cybersecurity leadership through the services and products rendered by Amazon Web Services and their cloud services, infrastructure, and platform. When coupled with AWS intrusion detection and intrusion presentation, the increased layer of security protects the EC2 instances used for cloud storage. The alerting administrator identifies attacks and takes action to control attacks. This approach supports institutions of higher education in stopping the threat of cyberattackers impeding their information systems when storage and usage of such applications and tools are in the cloud.

Furthermore, employing cryptology methods that secure information in transit and at rest is essential to supporting institutions of higher education, manage their risks of successful cyberattack incidents. The use of cryptology is not new. In fact, usage of cryptography messages dates to the early Greek era when messages were encoded. Polybios utilized a grid of letters, in which each letter in a message is replaced by two letters; this indicates the row and column that the original letter aligns with. Even though Suetonius assumed Caeser utilized this systematic approach, research conveys that Caesar replaced Latin letters with Greek letters in a way that was not made completely clear. [25] Stanford University reports that the two primary departments that affect cryptography are the National Institute of Standards and Technology and National Security Agency. In 1987, under the Computer Secrecy Act, the National Institute of Standards and Technology was selected to work with government agencies and private corporations to create security standards. While the NIST is still a leader in establishing these standards, the usage of cryptography is not enforced. Furthermore, the National Security Agency is obsessed with national security regulations, they continually block any exportation of cryptography technology utilized over the Internet. This cripples industries who seek to develop this technology. It is reported that the NSA's reasoning for forbidding export is a fear of terrorists' increased ability to utilize US encryption methods to encode threatening messages.

However, institutions of higher education need effective methods of encoding data in transit and data at rest. Implementing multiple techniques and methods of securing information is key to thwarting successful cyberattacks. Amazon Web Services continues evolving into the "go-to" service and product provider for institutions of higher education worldwide. After all, usage of data at rest encryption is the next phase of ensuring cybersecurity leadership is deployed correctly and effectively. AWS renders the necessary tools required to develop an encryption file system to encrypt all data assets and metadata at rest, utilizing an industry standard AES-256 encryption algorithm. [26] Encrypted file systems are developed to manage encryption and decryption automatically and transparently. Thus, institutions of higher education subject to regulatory policies also need to ensure encryption of data and metadata at rest occurs daily, and utilization of this file system becomes a norm. Working in partnership with AWS is one sure way institutions of higher education can outthink and outperform cybercriminals seeking to prey on their vulnerable information systems, technology tools, and software applications.

Another useful system of support for institutions of higher education is machine learning. Machine learning embodies three models: binary classification, which helps predict one of two possible outcomes; multi-class classification, which predicts one of more than two outcomes; and regression, which predicts a numeric value. [27] For example, usage of machine learning for institutions of higher education can help decrease the number of successful email phishing attempts that are often mishandled by executive leaders, administrators, faculty, and staff. Utilizing Amazon Machine Learning enables institutions of higher education to improve their prediction of phishing email, by collecting email examples correctly labeled as spam or not spam. Machine learning generalizes these email examples to predict how likely it is that institutions of higher education will receive new email phishing messages or not. This method of assessment enables improved learning from data that has been classified with actual answers and is known as supervised machine learning. [28]

And because cyberattacks are being deployed against institutions of higher education globally, usage of effective translation services and products that understand the natural language processing of information and data is crucial to supporting institutions of higher education worldwide. Having a reliable translation partnership can support institutions of higher education in better developing, implementing, and managing cybersecurity leadership, through recommendations and guidelines developed by the National Institute of Standards and Technology, the European Commission, and additional global Governments, who continually develop and update cybersecurity public policy to guide and protect public and private sector entities from cybercrime victimization.

Amazon Translate is a reliable service that will be a dynamic "go-to" for institutions of higher education, in search of a better way of understanding globalized language barriers. The broad language translation service works with 75 languages, including: Afrikaans, Albanian, Amharic, Arabic, Armenian, Azerbaijani, Bengali, Bosnian, Bulgarian, Chinese (Simplified), Catalan, Chinese (Traditional), Croatian, Czech, Danish, Dari, Dutch, English, Estonian, Finnish, French, French (Canada), Georgian, German, Greek, Gujarati, Haitian Creole, Hausa, Hebrew, Hindi, Hungarian, Icelandic, Indonesian, Irish, Italian, Japanese, Kannada, Kazakh, Korean, Latvian, Lithuanian, Macedonian, Malay, Malayalam, Maltese, Mongolian, Marathi, Norwegian, Farsi (Persian), Pashto, Polish, Portuguese, Portuguese (Portugal), Punjabi, Romanian, Russian, Serbian, Sinhala, Slovak, Slovenian, Somali, Spanish, Spanish (Mexico), Swahili, Swedish, Filipino Tagalog, Tamil, Telugu, Thai, Turkish, Ukrainian, Urdu, Uzbek, Vietnamese, and Welsh. [28]. This translation service also supports 5550 translation combinations. Using this as an automatic summarization and machine translate service, can help decrease the challenges that are commonly known with using machine translation service providers. You will gain additional information about AWS Translation services in another chapter.

3.2 Summary

Institutions of higher education are facing a tremendous battle thwarting and defending themselves against unwanted cyberattacks. Working under duress to stay current with trends in cyberattacks and the methods used by cybercriminals, is a daunting task that remains uncontrolled. When efforts are implemented to deter one approach of cyberattack, there are other cyberattack methods being created and deployed to outthink and outwit institutions of higher education. Governments worldwide are working endlessly to enact new laws to help control the growing central phenomenon of higher education cyberattack incidents. However, due to the limited ability to hire qualified, educated, and trained information systems and technology practitioners, who are knowledgeable of current trends in cybersecurity defense and cybercrime attack methods and approaches, many institutions of higher education will continue being victimized. Thus, this chapter provided some clarity on some current methods of strategy that are available for institutions of higher education to achieve improved cybersecurity attack performance. This chapter enables you to comprehend what level of security should be entrusted to protect institutions of higher education from cyberattack victimization. Unless there are recorded and documented proven results showing how one institution of higher education has controlled their victimization of cyberattack completely. Institutions of higher education will endure challenges trying to stay ahead of cybercriminals, who seem to remain sophisticated in vetting what vulnerabilities are readily penetrable at what institution. To help decrease this corrupt activity, institutions of higher education must rely on multiple resources, domestically and internationally, to improve cybersecurity resilience, mitigation, and intrusion prevention and detection. This chapter delivered clarity to invoke more research be done by institutions of higher education to better prepare for the future and to continue preventing successful cyberattacks from impacting the ability for these institutions to operate without fear of being victimized. Having this resource as a guide to understand what recommendations and guidelines are readily available for usage, should ensure you that cybersecurity leaders and experts are taking this threat seriously, and working endlessly to support your defense needs. Now is the time that institutions of higher education employ the same scale of effort and stop negating the seriousness of these cyberattack incidents. Otherwise, you risk losing economic stability and reputational damage.

3.3 Investigative Scenario

Benedictine University has been relying on Windows 7 professional operating system for the last eight years. Using this operating system is simple for all executive leaders and administrators to develop documents, store documents, and transmit documents to and from internal and external individuals and organizations. Active Directory has been useful in supporting the daily business operational needs and communication for the university. However, recently some of the executive leaders, i.e., deans and provost, have been targeted with phishing emails. Details regarding the last email incident, included the dean of English receiving an email transmitted with an email address from an internal constituent, which it was assumed was a legitimate email address and message. The email message requested the dean to share sensitive details about students in his program. Information included students names and students identification numbers. The dean unwittingly responded to the email request and sent over details of all students in the program, consisting of 50 students from both the current semester and the previous. When the dean met up with the assumed sender of the email and began discussing the content of the email, the receiver was discombobulated, and unsure what he was referring to. The dean insisted that he'd shared the information and sent it in response to the email. After examination of the actual email sent over, there was evidence proving the email was sent from an external sub netted email IP address. Although an investigation was conducted, and the dean and his constituents were informed of the potential risk of responding and opening emails that are being sent by assumed personnel. The institution failed to provide training to prepare the executive leaders to help improve deterrence of these threats.

One way this event could have been thwarted is working in partnership with the third-party service provider Amazon Web Services, which renders quality encryption cloud services that support higher education institutions from cybercrime victimization. Amazon Web Services partners with Perception Point that offers increased interception of all content-based attack methods across collaborative channels, including email and messaging platforms. This service provider also is known for preventing phishing, BEC, spam, malware, zero-day attacks, and N-day attacks. They profess to have the ability to stop attacks prior to attacks reaching their proposed target. Usage of this application is supported by the United States Cybersecurity & Infrastructure Security Agency. Although not endorsing this service provider, the CISA conveys that Perception Point's Free eMail Security Plan, provides organizations security from any threat entering an organization's email system and additional collaborative channels. To learn more, log on to https://www.cisa.gov/cross-sector-cybersecurity-performance-goals

3.4 Discussion Questions

1. Why did the European Commission mandate the General Data Protection Regulation (GDPR)?
2. What 157-year-old private college closed its doors permanently after being targeted by a ransomware attack?
3. What ransomware gang successfully targeted North Carolina A&T State University in 2022?

4. In May 2021, what country's universities were successfully targeted with cyberattacks and what type of cyberattacks?
5. In 2022, the University of Neuchâtel was successfully targeted due to what known vulnerability?
6. What known dangerous organization deployed a sophisticated cyberattack using social engineering techniques to access public intellectuals in the Middle East?
7. What was the value of the ransomware attack deployed against the University of the West of Scotland?
8. When is digital leadership evident?
9. What does digital competence and culture mean?
10. Who was selected to work with government agencies and private corporations to create security standards?

Glossary

Algorithm – a process or set of rules used in calculations and additional problem-solving operations, particularly in computers.

CIA triad – standards mandated by the National Institute of Standards and Technology to impose ethical practice of confidentiality, integrity, and availability on information security.

Cryptology – controlled by the National Institute of Standards and Technology to increase layers of encryption and methods of decryption of sensitive information assets.

Digital infrastructure – when institutions of higher education possess knowledge and embody intelligence to effectively access, connect, and utilize all technology, including physical equipment, software, and technical support services rendered by third-party service and product providers, needed to enable daily operation of business and communication across the institution to benefit from the integration of the digital conversion.

Digital leadership – when institutions of higher education possess a comprehensive and strategic outlook for technology integration at all scales of the institution's needs and capacity, to effectively implement technology as a key component to managing and delivering services and products.

Distributed denial of service attack – a malicious cyberattack targeting a website interface to flood the network to prevent accessibility.

Human error – mismanagement and usage of computer software and hardware that enables cyberattackers to gain access to a secured network or information system to deploy nefarious activity.

Phishing attack – deceitful attempt to disguise information as a known identifiable individual to gain access to sensitive information to be used for nefarious reasons.

Man-in-the-middle attack – a nefarious act of intercepting transmitted information sent across the Internet from a sender to receiver who modifies or distorts details of the original message for malicious purpose.

Social engineering – a nefarious activity used to ask pertinent questions to gain useful information regarding sensitive details on people and places for monetary gain or malicious activity.

TA453 – a dangerous Iranian hacking cyber gang who deploys malicious cyberattacks on vulnerable institutions of higher education to exploit their network and information system for monetary gain.

Trojan – a computer virus created to enable hackers to send messages encoded with malicious code that is wittingly installed on a computer device to infect the data files and information system.

Whaling – a targeted cyberattack designed for executive leaders, disguised to impersonate a colleague to acquire access to sensitive data assets for monetary gain.

References

[1] Bank of America, (2023) High ed is top target for cyber criminals. [PDF] Retrieved from: https://business.bofa.com/content/dam/flagship/gcb/keeping-institutions-safe/keeping_instititutions_safe.pdf

[2] Gregory, J. (2022, October 12). Ransomware attacks target U.S. colleges and universities. [Website] Retrieved from: https://securityintelligence.com/news/ransomware-attackers-target-us-colleges-universities/

[3] Avertium, (2022, June 7). The Top 5 Cyber Threats Within the Education Sector. [Website] Retrieved from: https://explore.avertium.com/resource/top-5-cyber-threats-within-education

[4] Diamantakos, R. (2021, May 27). Higher education institutions in Canada can now share cybersecurity threats internationally. [Website] Retrieved from: https://www.ctvnews.ca/sci-tech/higher-education-institutions-in-canada-can-now-share-cybersecurity-threats-internationally-1.5446087

[5] Cox, A. (2023, July 28). Scottish university UWS targeted by cyber attackers. [Website] Retrieved from: https://www.bbc.com/news/uk-scotland-glasgow-west-66327336

[6] Euronews, (2021, May 5). Belgium's parliament and universities hit by cyber-attack. [Website] Retrieved from: https://www.euronews.com/2021/05/05/belgium-s-parliament-and-universities-hit-by-cyber-attack

[7] SWO swissinfo.ch (2022, February 19). University of Neuchâtel back online after cyberattack. [Website] Retrieved from: https://www.swissinfo.ch/eng/business/university-of-neuch%C3%A2tel-hit-by-cyberattack/47360432

[8] SWO swissinfo.ch (2023, February 3). Hackers target Zurich university with 'professional' cyberattack. [Website] Retrieved from: https://www.swissinfo.ch/eng/sci-tech/hackers-target-zurich-university-with-professional-cyberattack/48256306

[9] Whalebone, (2021, August 30). Universities Pay Significant Ransomware in Case of a Cyberattack or Lose Valuable Information about Their Students and research. [Website] Retrieved from: https://www.whalebone.io/post/universities-pay-significant-ransom-in-case-of-a-cyberattack-or-lose-valuable-information-about-their-students-and-research

[10] OECD (2023, April), Advancing Digital Maturity in Croatia's Higher Education System, Higher Education, OECD Publishing, Paris. [PDF] Retrieved from: https://www.oecd-ilibrary.org/docserver/c3c8d452-en.pdf?expires=1708084123&id=id&accname=guest&checksum=7C736B6E085FF8AE856BD50B7ABC6202

[11] National Institute of Standards and Technology, (2012, September). Information Security. [PDF] Retrieved from: https://csrc.nist.gov/pubs/sp/800/30/r1/final

[12] Torriera-Mikolic, I., Henry, R., Snyder, D., Beaghley, S., Pettyjohn, L.S., Harting, S., Westerman, E., Shlapak, A.D., Bishop, M., Oberholtzer, J., Skrabala, L. & Weinbaum, C. (2016). A Framework for Exploring Cybersecurity Policy Options. [PDF] Retrieved from: https://www.rand.org/content/dam/rand/pubs/research_reports/RR1700/RR1700/RAND_RR1700.pdf

[13] Newhouse, W., Keith, S., Scribner, B. & Witte, G. (2017, August). National Initiative for Cybersecurity Education (NICE) Cybersecurity Workforce Framework. [PDF] Retrieved from: https://doi.org/10.6028/NIST.SP.800-181

[14] Chiou, S., (2013, May 15). Secure Methods for Biometric-Based Recognition with Integrated Cryptographic Functions. [Website] Retrieved from: https://www.ncbi.nlm.nih.gov/pmc/articles/PMC3671241/

[15] Committee on National Security Systems, (2010). Committee on National Security Systems National Information Assurance (IA)

Glossary. [PDF] Retrieved from: http://www.cnss.gov/Assets/pdf/cnssi_4009.pdf

[16] National Center of Education Statistics, (1998). Protecting Your System: Information Security. [Website] retrieved from: https://nces.ed.gov/pubs98/safetech/chapter6.asp

[17] Federal Information Security Modernization Act, (n.d.). What is FISMA? [Website] Retrieved from: https://security.cms.gov/learn/federal-information-security-modernization-act-fisma

[18] Kurtz, L. (2023, April 10). Can getting rid of passwords stop ransomware in higher education? [Website] Retrieved from: https://doubleoctopus.com/blog/passwordless-mfa/can-getting-rid-of-passwords-stop-ransomware-in-higher-education/

[19] National Institute of Standards and Technology, (2012, August). Computer Security Incident Handling Guide. [Website] retrieved from: https://csrc.nist.gov/pubs/sp/800/61/r2/final

[20] U.S. Department of Health and Human Services, (2023, October 12). Cybersecurity Incident Response Plans. [PDF] Retrieved from: https://www.hhs.gov/sites/default/files/cybersecurity-incident-response-plans.pdf

[21] Cybersecurity & Infrastructure Security Agency, (n.d.). Incident Response Training. [Website] Retrieved from: https://www.cisa.gov/resources-tools/programs/Incident-Response-Training

[22] RiskOptics, (2023, August 3). Security Misconfigurations: Definition, Causes, and Avoidance Strategies. [Website] Retrieved from: https://reciprocity.com/blog/security-misconfigurations-how-to-avoid-them/

[23] Amorosa, K. & Yankson, B. (2023, June). Human Error-A Critical Contributing Factor to the Rise in Data Breaches: A Case Study of Higher Education. [PDF] Retrieved from: https://www.researchgate.net/publication/371849122_Human_Error_-_A_Critical_Contributing_Factor_to_the_Rise_in_Data_Breaches_A_Case_Study_of_Higher_Education

[24] Amazon Web Services, (2024). Intrusion Detection & Intrusion Prevention. [Website] Retrieved from: https://aws.amazon.com/mp/scenarios/security/ids/

[25] Stanford University, (n.d.). Public Key Cryptography. [Website] Retrieved from: https://cs.stanford.edu/people/eroberts/courses/soco/projects/public-key-cryptography/main.html

[26] Amazon Web Services, (2024). Encryption of Data at Rest. [Website] Retrieved from: https://docs.aws.amazon.com/whitepapers/latest/efs-encrypted-file-systems/encryption-of-data-at-rest.html

[27] Amazon Web Services, (2024). Solving Business Problems with Amazon Machine Learning. [Website] Retrieved from: https://docs.aws.amazon.com/machine-learning/latest/dg/machine-learning-problems-in-amazon-machine-learning.html

[28] Amazon Web Services, (2024). Benefits of Amazon Translate. [Website] https://aws.amazon.com/translate/

4

Penetration Testing

Learning Objectives

- Interpret the history of penetration testing.
- Distinguish current trends in penetration testing.
- Construct and formulate penetration testing for healthcare organizations and institutions of higher education.
- Summarize auditing strategies to improve IT security and policy compliance.

4.1 Introduction

In 2006, the Sans Institute published an intelligence report titled *Penetration Testing: Assessing Your Overall Security Before Attackers Do*, authored by Stephen Northcutt, Jerry Shenk, Dave Shackleford, Tim Rosenberg, Raul Siles, and Steve Mancini. This report provides an impeccable understanding of what penetration testing is, why penetration testing should be performed, and shares details explaining pen-testing tools and methods of reporting. Since this report's publishing dissemination, the number of healthcare organizations and institutions of higher education, who have suffered cyberattacks globally, has risen exponentially. The number of information system and information technology practitioners working in healthcare organizations and institutions of higher education has increased, but not enough to outnumber the successful cyberattack actors deploying these malicious attacks. And although, there is conversation to increase knowledge awareness and training regarding cyberattack incidents; the ability to outline a plan to effectively improve the approach and management of cybersecurity leadership in healthcare organizations and institutions of higher education, remain entrenched in ineffective planning, lack of guidance on methods of auditing, and inefficient measures of penetration testing. Three of the most useful methods of assessing a network for vulnerabilities are conducting vulnerability assessments, auditing, and penetration testing. Penetration testing has gained popularity because of the effective results this form of cybersecurity assessment provides. Research explains that implementing penetration testing can be beneficial in a university's IT infrastructure and services. [1] Since universities are relying on website interface engagement, internally and externally, implementing methods to audit and test for vulnerabilities woven in the information system, can help lower the increased probability of a successful cyberattack.

Thus, the research in this chapter derives from Michael E. Whitman and Herbert J. Mattord, two information security authors and industry experts, who report that vulnerability assessments should be accompanied by penetration testing. [2] This chapter provides a look into Woeson Books, an eCommerce company who was victimized by a cyberattack. This research provides an understanding why vulnerability assessments are important and help you learn what type of vulnerabilities were discovered, and how penetration testing played a role in helping discover these vulnerabilities, to help determine the type of mitigation and patch efforts required to increase cybersecurity leadership. You will also learn about some of the penetration testing tools utilized and how these tools are instrumental in supporting cybersecurity leadership. Furthermore, you will learn how to assess AWS for healthcare organizations and institutions higher education as a reliable service and product application provider and partner for effective auditing and penetration testing. An investigative scenario is provided and a summary of this chapter, including discussion questions.

The history of penetration testing began when the U.S. Department of Defense and the military began examining the importance of assessing software for vulnerabilities. Historically, the "Tiger Team" was responsible for examining computer networks to locate security vulnerabilities, which eventually evolved into pen testing. [3] Not shortly after this discovery, the National Institute of Standards and Technology (NIST) introduced several special series publications, including NIST SP 800-95 Guide to Secure Web Services, NIST SP 800-12 Rev. 1 An Introduction to Information Security, NIST SP 800-53 Rev.5 Security and Privacy Controls for Information Systems and Organizations, NIST SP 800-137 Information Security, NIST SP 800-115 Technical Guide to Information Security Testing and Assessment, NIST SP 800-152 A Profile for U.S. Federal Cryptographic Key Management Systems, and NIST SP 800-160v1r1 Engineering Trustworthy Secure Systems. Each one of these publications render clear and concise recommendations and guidelines on methods of preparing and deploying penetration testing for systems and enables network security administrators and cybersecurity practitioners to gain essential knowledge on the significant role penetration testing plays in helping thwart successful cyberattacks. However, even with these tools and guidelines available, many healthcare organizations and institutions of higher education do not have the quality team of information system and information technology practitioners, who are aware of how to assess and audit their systems effectively or utilize penetration testing tools to patch system vulnerabilities, or how to implement improved methods and strategies to deter cyberattacks. Thus, this research shares clarity on the role of auditing as it relates to penetration testing.

Penetration testing has two phases – internal and external. Internal penetration testing embodies continued assessment of an institution's internal network, system, and data security using penetration testing. Today, internal penetration testing has grown into continuous internal penetration testing (CIPT). This means, institutions of higher education and healthcare organizations should be implementing and assessing penetration testing. The objectives of CIPT are to determine known vulnerabilities, weaknesses, and potential gateway entrance points that could become exploitable by external malicious attack agents. [4] External penetration testing involves contractors or consultants, who are known as white-hat hackers, ethical hackers, black-hat hackers, or gray-hat hackers. Ethical hacking is a legal action of authorized intrusion into a computer system network or web interface application to test the strength and risks of vulnerabilities, to determine if those vulnerabilities are penetrable. Permission is granted by an organization to allow this ethical intrusion to occur to improve plans and strategies of deterring successful cyberattacks. Ethical hackers try to bypass system security to locate weak points to exploit them before malicious hackers do. The information attained during this testing enables organizations to improve their system security. This also helps eliminate potential attacks. [5]

White-hat hackers are good hackers, who use their hacking abilities for defense purposes. White-hat hackers are often security professionals who possess the knowledge of hacking and understand hacker tools that help discover weaknesses and know how to implement effective countermeasures. Black-hat hackers are the bad guys. They invade network servers and information systems to violate system integrity, using remote access and possess malicious intent. Black-hat hackers want to destroy pertinent data, stop access to web interfaces by authorized end users, and cause issues for their target. Black-hat hackers are differentiated from white-hat hackers because white-hat hackers do not have intent to do harm. Gray-hat hackers are self-proclaimed ethical hackers, who focus on hacker tools with a childlike curiosity. They often desire to highlight security flaws in a system to educate their victims, to encourage their victims to increase security of their system effectively. A few years ago, I gained the opportunity to be a gray-hat hacker for Woeson Books, who relied on a website interface to conduct eBusiness, which includes rendering services and products and collecting payments using a Wi-Fi accessible payment system.

During my initial assessment, I discovered that Woeson Books utilized Microsoft servers and PCs and a few Mac computers to perform design work. I also learned that they use Active Directory, and have IIS Web server for their Internet website, including two Microsoft Exchange servers being used to process their corporate email. Furthermore, I learned, they have four servers they're using as file shares; one server is located at each of their physical office locations, i.e., China, Hong Kong, Japan, and Taiwan. Woeson Books possess four additional servers for hosting their internal billing inventory, CRM, and employee applications. Plus, they have one training server and 5 MS SQL backend database servers.

Woeson Books network is located behind a gateway router and firewall with the implementation of third-party antivirus software, which is not automatically updated across all the organization's PCs. Woeson Books is utilizing Windows Server Update Services to update Windows servers and client PCs. However, like their antivirus software, not everything encompassing their network web applications is updated regularly. In addition, I learned that some employees often work remotely and tend to utilize their login and passwords to attain access to the corporate network. Additionally, I discovered Woeson Books outsources their email spam and human resource applications to two separate third-party companies. The IT department operates with six full-time employees, including the director of IT. However, one of five full-time employees also works in IT security for Woeson Books, part-time. And even though there is due diligence demonstrated by the security staff at their physical office, each office has mixed results in their level of security.

The owners of Woeson Books realized their IT infrastructure and organization has some known problems, especially since PCs and additional office equipment were recently stolen from their main office in China. It's suspected that this incident occurred after two employees recently left and joined their biggest competitor – Wang Chang Books. Recently, there was a breach on Woeson Books website, where credit card information, book orders, account numbers, and addresses of customers were retrieved. Woeson Books sought suggestions on how to redefine their current website security features. Some suggestions that were provided included auditing the system regularly and developing and implementing information security policies to better control risk management. Penetration testing was recommended to

Table 4.1 FAIR threat event frequency.

Level	Description
Extremely low	Lowest 2% when compared against the overall threat population
Low	Bottom 16% when compared against the overall threat population
Moderate	Between 1 and 10 times per year
High	Between 10 and 100 times per year
Very high	Greater 100 times per year

help improve and maintain security risk levels of the website. This includes evaluating for malware and viruses.

As acting cybersecurity leader, my initial step involved measuring Woeson Books security posture against the security standards enacted by National Institute of Standards of Technology (NIST). According to the NIST, risk assessments are an invaluable part of effective risk management and should include the organization level, mission/business process level, and information system level. [6] It is recommended that because risk management is an ongoing process, risk assessments must be deployed in compliance with current systematic development cycles, beginning with a pre-system acquisition to a system acquisition, and prior transitioning into sustainment. Each risk assessment must be defined by the size and circumstances of the organization or business scale of threat, i.e., high, middle, or low. This should include utilizing various formats, styles of charts, tables, and content associated with reporting mechanisms because healthcare organizations and institutions of higher education embody unique flexibility in how they approach risk assessments.

Table 4.1 provides clarity on the measurement frequency. The FAIR threat event frequency methodology was selected as a tool to measure the security posture because this provides a very comprehensive framework for analyzing information risks, including a step-by-step process for qualifying risks. [7] This model of risk assessment offers a unique way of breaking risk down into various phases, while maintaining simple analysis configuration. This model can be applied to qualitative and quantitative analysis.

The objective was to measure the vulnerabilities and threats using the FAIR threat event frequency table. This is important because to effectively calculate vulnerability variables-i.e., human error and outdated software, with the threat event frequency-i.e., extremely high, high, medium or low, determines the loss event frequency-i.e., reputational damage, monetary loss, required to compare the strength capability of the threat source-i.e., outdated software with the strength of the existing risks controls implemented-i.e., Firewall, intrusion detection intrusion prevention software, used to prevent a successful exploitation. [8] The second objective is to utilize a practical method to estimate losses, to provide ranges rather than identifying a precise value. The appropriate ranges will be different depending on if the organization is a healthcare organization or an institution of higher education. Thus, this table would be modified for whatever unique entity. The third objective is to effectively qualify all factors that impact the probability and severity of each risk discovered. Utilizing this model is a dynamic way to approach a detailed analysis of vulnerabilities. When this approach was deployed on behalf of Woeson Books offices, information security posture, the vulnerability assessment included the following focus areas:

- Windows Embedded Standard, i.e., two Windows Embedded XP, two Windows Embedded 7
- two Windows Server 2008 R2 for Embedded Systems
- two Windows Server 2012 R2 for Embedded Systems – e.g., 24 systems running Jet Direct
- five network applications running embedded Linux
- hardware
- software
- confidentially and privacy policies
- physical inspection
- website servers
- email servers
- network infrastructure
- network topologies

4.2 Very High-level Findings

- Windows Embedded XP lacks service update availability since Microsoft discontinued extending support for this system in 2016 – when they discontinued "service pack" up-date support for the Windows XP OS. Due to this, intrusion via hacking is possible because patching on embedded operating systems is a problem. This is because general-purpose and embedded operating systems utilize drivers to interface with hardware devices. Both types of OSs drivers are vulnerable to exploitation and need to be consistently updated and patched.
- Vulnerabilities were discovered in Windows 7. To combat this, it is recommended to utilize a Microsoft Security Only Quality Update

and Security Monthly Quality Rollup. However imperative to understand there is a remote code execution vulnerability and information disclosure vulnerability that could be launched against the system. For instance, if a hacker gained the same privileges as a logged-on employee or staff, he/she could install malicious software, i.e., keylogger or malware, and view, modify, and delete information as well as create new accounts with complete user rights. Therefore, it was recommended to maintain updates as Microsoft suggest.

- A vulnerability was discovered with the Windows Server 2012 R2 for Embedded Systems. Patches that mitigate such vulnerability are available through manual download for Microsoft Windows operating systems. Microsoft recommended disabling SMBv1 on all systems and relying on SMBv2 or SMBv3. It was also recommended all Woeson Books employees be reminded not to visit untrusted websites and/or follow links embedded in emails from unknown sources. This is highly normal in healthcare organizations and institutions of higher education, where phishing email attacks are deployed and often the reason ransomware attacks are integrated. Researching the Common Vulnerabilities and Exposure website to learn about the vulnerabilities in software applications is beneficial.

4.3 Security Program

The existing security program implemented internally at Woeson Books includes usage of Microsoft servers and PCs, with a few Mac computers utilized to perform design work. It also includes (1) Active Directory; IIS web server for Internet website; (2) Microsoft Exchange servers for processing corporate emails; (3) servers utilized as file shares (e.g., one-per office), (4) servers utilized for housing internal billing, inventory, and CRM, and employee applications plus, utilization of a training server; and (5) MS SQL backend database servers.

There were five Windows 2008 servers in the main office, two were remote accessible, three were physical servers. System updates and patches were being run from the main office and systems receive Microsoft updates monthly; even though, some updates were missed. The usage of third-party products (e.g., Adobe Acrobat Reader) was not kept up to date, and all employees are conducting daily business tasks on a desktop or laptop PCs running Windows 7. Unfortunately, Windows 7 updates were not being configured automatically, which provides an entrance for cyberattackers to exploit Woeson Books operating system.

The current network sits behind a gateway router and firewall. Antivirus is in use but is not automatically updated across all company PCs. Windows Server Update Services is configured to update Windows servers and client PCs, but like antivirus software, not everything gets updated regularly. Furthermore, employees tend to work remotely and use their login and password to gain access to the corporate systems. Woeson Books outsources their email spam and all human resource applications to two separate third-party companies. It is unsure if these third-party service providers are aligning business practices with the GDPR, and not sharing these sensitive resources with other third-party service providers for monetary gain. Woeson Books also utilizes an IIS web server for their website. Since older versions of IIS web server utilize various features by default, this leaves room for attack. Research explains that Microsoft designed the IIS Lockdown Wizard for locking down IIS versions 4.0 and 5.0. This can be downloaded from Microsoft support.

4.4 Recommendations for Improvement

- All installed software application must be updated regularly as recommended by the software developer. Systems should be configured to enable automatic updates on all employee computers, networks, and devices. This must include Internet browser and Microsoft software applications.
- Firewall and antivirus software should be updated and reviewed bi-monthly for potential vulnerabilities.
- All embedded OSs need to be assessed and proper updates rendered to countermeasure vulnerabilities. This should be assessed in compliance with CVE (common vulnerability exposures), utilizing the CVE site, i.e., http://www.cve.mitre.org
- Security compliance policy should be modified and shared with all employees at all locations, and training should be provided to enforce compliance across all departments. Employees should be made aware of all security policies and security practices. There should be assessments done to measure employees' knowledge regarding security policy compliance, quarterly.

4.5 Nine-step Task to Implement Effective Information Security

- *System profiling* – information flows are identified, and risk measures are rated; identify any functionality, data classifications, and system/user interactions.

- *Requirements* – baseline security measures are established, and necessary enhancements are determined.
- *Control selection* – controls are selected in correlation to the functional requirements identified in the previous step.
- *Risk exposure analysis* – establishes current level of risk exposure calculated for each flow.
- *Control validation and placement* – control design validated, and security value measured.
- *Document risk decisions* – utilizing results from risk data and functionality requirements to support risk management decisions in compliance with approved risk management procedures.
- *Implement* – effective integration of all agreed policy plans and modifications identified throughout the assessment process.
- *Assessment* – this should include gathering evidence that support controls and ensuring implementation is effective and controls are operating as required. This includes validating controls implemented to provide correct outcomes and ensure security requirements are met. This should include providing clearly written reports explaining discovered evidence of vulnerabilities to decision makers, who can make firm decisions on what countermeasures should be implemented to eliminate vulnerabilities.
- *Monitoring and auditing* – deploying an ongoing performance evaluation should be practiced ensuring new implementations are maintaining control effectively and efficiently.

4.6 Key Security Recommendations

- Firewalls must be updated and configured effectively.
- Software updates must be configured for automatic updating according to each software manufacturer.
- Network firewalls must be configured effectively, and updates should be configured correctly.
- All employee PCs must be configured for updates and security threat evaluations.
- Employee mobile devices must be secured to configure with remote access to Woeson Books network to minimize risk to the network.

- Embedded OS vulnerabilities must be patched.
- Woeson Book's website must be assessed for patches and security socket layers of encryption – SSL/TLS, must be applied to all web pages.
- Network ports that remain open, but not in use, must be closed.
- Woeson Books must maintain an effective information security policy that mirrors NIST standards.

4.7 Action Plan

- Regular meetings with IT and human resource managers to discuss current information security policies within the organization and to update those that need updating.
- Define new information security policies that mirror standards recommended by NIST Special Publication 800-115.
- Correlate with manufacturer of firewall system applications and software applications, to configure remote scheduled updates as recommended by the service provider.
- Install security socket layer certifications on the Woeson Books website to ensure sensitive data is encrypted.
- Network access control had to be implemented to add additional security internally.
- There was a need to enforce repercussions for employee noncompliance with information security policies.
- It is determined that employees must be trained in all technology upgrades within Woeson Books.
- It is determined that IT managers and staff should be evaluated for certification requirements and required to complete continued education training, including attending annual conferences and cybersecurity expos, worldwide, to stay current with trends in cybersecurity leadership.

4.8 Detailed System Findings

During the assessment it was determined Woeson Books website lacked security layer certifications, which enabled access to sensitive data. This was rated a high-level security risk that must be addressed immediately. It was also determined that Woeson Books firewall applications were not being updated and managed effectively. This, too, was a high-level security risk factor. There was no well-defined security policy implemented and relied on, which was a high-level security risk. Thus, it was determined that a security policy be developed, assessed, implemented, and monitored monthly, to ensure compliance is practiced throughout the organization. All PCs must be configured with updated security settings and updates should be installed on all software applications. No default passwords should be utilized. Written reports should be kept on file to record report dates and convey when updates were conducted and explain how information should be stored and secured in file systems with encryption controls. All embedded OSs must be evaluated, and research should be conducted to ensure that OSs are being effectively updated. Reports must be written out clearly to convey all steps taken to protect the operating system relied on. And web servers and network servers must be updated with any security feature that will install additional layers of security. Written reports must be kept regarding these installations to effectively record activities implemented and practiced. And all open ports on the network must be kept closed to prevent potential risk of unauthorized intrusion.

4.9 Scoring Information

The score indicator listed below provides a metric for how Woeson Books measured overall in compliance with ISO 27001 guidelines.

High or Red = represents a serious security finding that could be exploited and damage customers' trust in the services rendered by Woeson Books.

Medium or Yellow = represents a security finding that may pose a risk to the customer but is not currently exploitable.

No Risk or Green = represents a good finding in which there are no risks to the customer.

High	Middle	No Risk
Windows Embedded XP lacks service update availability	No security policy has been developed	Embedded OS configuration and updates
Vulnerability discovered in Windows Embedded 7		
Woeson Books website lacks security layer certification		

High	Middle	No Risk
Ports open on network	PCs must be configured with default security settings	
Webserver, email server, and network patches required		
Firewall application and software	Employee security compliance	

Keep in mind that relying on third-party applications requires maintaining ongoing communication that enable both healthcare organizations and institutions of higher education to stay up to date on manufacturer's recommendations regarding patches and mitigation strategies that must be deployed to maintain security of all known vulnerabilities discovered. Using OWASP is a dynamic way to assess vulnerabilities as well as CVE.mitre.org. Lacking the knowledge to access this valuable information will impact the success rate of successful vulnerability assessments. Using auditing tools and framework can also play a role in how effective vulnerability assessments are. While using penetration testing impacts the ability to ensure vulnerabilities are mitigated before cyberattackers learn about the known vulnerabilities in current software being utilized. However, it is important to consider what type of penetration testing tool that can help support healthcare organizations or institutions of higher education in completing vulnerability assessments.

Today, there are several known penetration testing tools that can be instrumental in supporting healthcare organizations and institutions of higher education. Nmap, Perl, and Wireshark are three tools that should be assessed to determine how each tool can be used for effective penetration testing within your organization. Perl can be used by security penetration testers to identify information about a remote computer. Perl can be used to automate or create tools to enable security testers to do security testing. Usage of Perl for security can also log parsing each day and is great for system hardening and system monitoring. When penetration testing, Perl enables network layer testing and the ability to conduct application layer testing. Perl also enables web application testing, fuzzing, and the ability to assess buffer overflow. Perl can also be useful for web vulnerability scanning and is instrumental for simple TCP port scanning. Additionally, exploits can be developed using Perl such as Metasploit helper (< 1.8). This helps locate length of a vulnerable buffer and can be useful in generating buffer with Perl assisting script. Perl is also useful for deploying a debugger.

Nmap is an open-source application that also is useful for penetration testing. You can access Nmap using the link provided: https://nmap.org/download.html. Once you install this application, you can scan your local network. The embedded image provides an example of the Zenmap primary screen after installation is completed. As you can see, the IP address is listed as the Target. You should input the computer device(s) IP address that you want to run a test on.

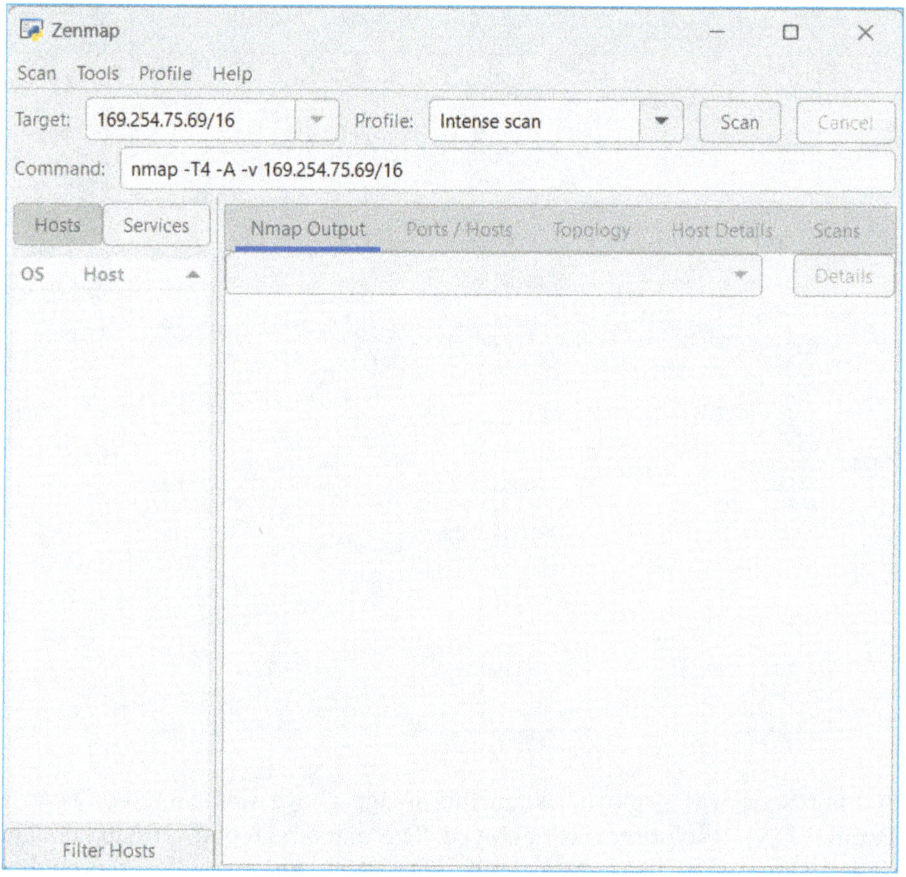

The type of scan you want to deploy can be determined by selecting from the drop-down menu next to Profile. For this example, I selected Intense scan. The results reported the following output:

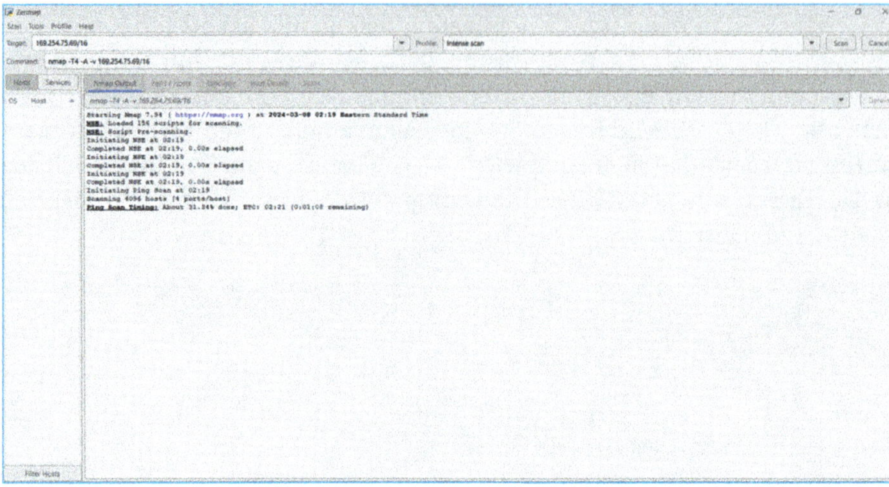

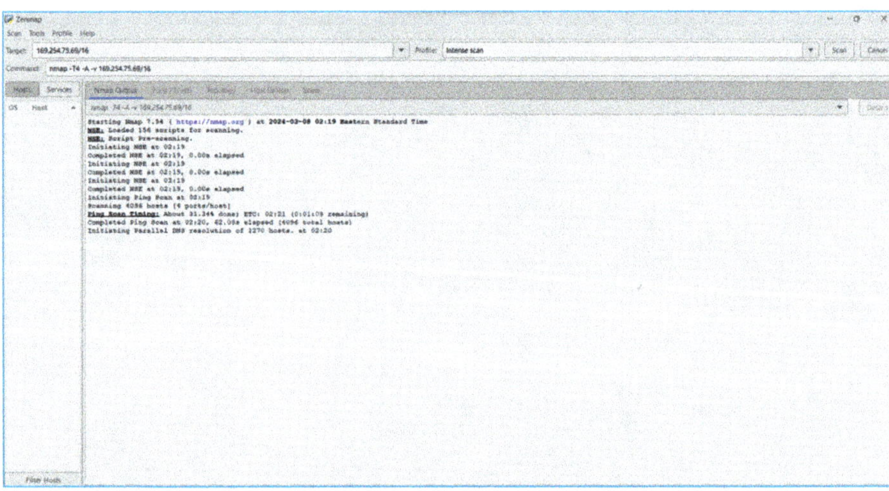

A Ping Scan was deployed when this image above was captured. Then a Parallel DNS resolution was deployed. The outcome reports Nmap host are down. Open ports were discovered. Then the scan continued, thoroughly assessing additional vulnerabilities. The image below provides details of what each scan discovered:

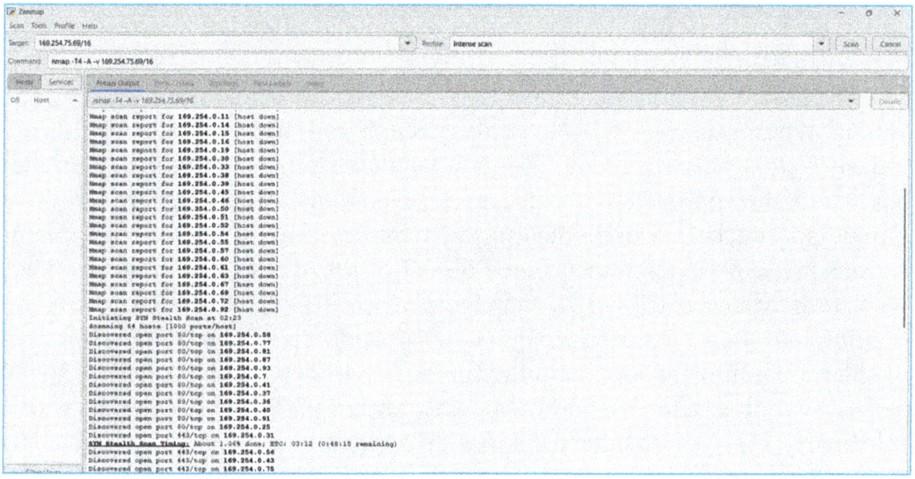

When I deploy a topology using a legend command, a pop-up screen shares a report of the host, trace route connections, and shares details of additional host icons, i.e., router, switches, wireless account points, and firewall. You can gain details regarding various scans and assess the ports that are opened and determine if these ports are vulnerable entrance points into the system. Taking time to understand Zenmap is essential to conducting a reliable penetration test of your device(s) to ensure configuration settings are current and impenetrable. Zenmap can be applied to various operating systems, including Windows, Linux, and Mac.

Wireshark can be accessed at https://www.wireshark.org/download.html. Knowing how this penetration testing tool applies to your testing needs is essential to utilizing it effectively. Wireshark provides thorough inspection of protocols and render live capture and offline analysis. [9] Wireshark can be deployed on Windows, Linux, and other systems. Wireshark can read/write many file types, including tcpdump, Pcap, Microsoft network monitor, network general sniffer, Net Screen snoop, and others. Wireshark provides decryption support for various protocols, including IPsec Kerberos, SSL/TCP, and WPZ/WPA2. Wireshark offers an online training platform through its Wireshark University, which can be accessed at https://www.wireshark.org/learn. [10] Usage of these tools is beneficial. However, it is important to understand each step you must deploy to conduct effective penetration testing, when using either application.

Research explains there are two strategies to penetrating testing, i.e., testing types utilized and the strategy deployed. Because the healthcare industry experience different cyberattack incidents than institutions of higher education, the approach to cybersecurity leadership differs. This requires two unique approaches to implementing penetration testing. Healthcare organizations are experiencing distributed denial of service attacks, targeting their website interface and Internet management consoles, where consumers are logging into their medical accounts to access and view their blood results, or to share vital information, including insurance information, birth date, social security number, address, and medical information. When partnering with a third-party service provider for software application, either for medical file storage and access or financial accounting, accountability of actions is vital to controlling risk embedded in each vulnerability integrated, engulfing each software application relied on.

Thus, it is important to implement a strategy to test the website interface using a penetration testing tool. But testing tools are not the only scale of security to be considered. Testing must be done on personnel as well. Personnel utilize the information system and information technology to retrieve medical files and to store those files. Encryption must be applied when files are uploaded and saved in the network server. Encryption should be advanced encryption standard at 256 impenetrable symmetric algorithms, reliant on a 256-bit key that converts plain text into cipher.

Multi-factor authentication login and password updated policy must be applied and utilized as outlined and intended in policy. This adds a layer of security that ensures that external attack actors cannot gain access to sensitive information. Information updates must be made as necessary to stay current with modifications. Policy must remain aligned with standards implemented by government recommendations and guidelines. Testing personnel must include assessing their knowledge of these requirements through procedural exams and comprehensive testing, i.e., multiple choice questions.

Software must be updated as recommended by the manufacturer. Staying aware of the service license agreement and ensuring the service provider is staying in alignment with that agreement, provides equity and confidentiality entrenched in integrity, meeting the CIA triad requirements. Software must be assessed for vulnerabilities and updated with recommended patches outlined by the U.S. Department of Defense. Knowing how to research the Common Vulnerability and Exposure database can save funding and reduce cyber incidents. Neglecting to do so can result in systems being exploited and a rise in cost for repair. Healthcare organizations have a higher number of consumers accessing and utilizing the eMedical file, than any institution of higher education. This increases the risk of potential victimization when end users lack the knowledge to access their medical records on a secure network effectively. The variables that must be assessed require usage of an organized infrastructure that should be adhered to and managed effectively.

Research explains that implementing one of three penetration testing models, i.e., physical structure, logical structure, or workflow of the system, can serve the needs of effective penetration testing for healthcare organizations or institutions of higher education. The physical structure involves assessing the building and campus of the medical center or organization where primary servers are located and financial office records are stored. These systems embody information assets that should be protected. When these assets are stored in cloud storage, security is applied to ensure confidentiality of those records. Penetration testing involves ensuring all OSHA and HIPAA laws are adhered to, implemented, and respected by personnel. Violators of HIPAA law can increase financial cost and liabilities for the healthcare organization. Thus, it is important that consistent training be rendered to increase compliance with the enforced regulations HIPAA governs.

The Gramm–Leach–Bliley Act, General Data Protection Act, California Children's Data Privacy Act, and many other policies enacted worldwide are essential management organization infrastructures that must be adhered to and implemented to meet the technology needs of the organization. When there is a disregard for the regulating policy, mismanagement becomes normal procedure and people are not held accountable for their negligence. Implementing physical penetration testing must include assessing the security of telecommunications for vulnerabilities and patching those vulnerabilities often discovered in VoIP, printers, copy machines, access key cards of doors, and entrance point key systems. Also, Wi-Fi network passwords are provided as default. However, it is recommended to change the default password to a new password and update the password every 45 days to ensure consistent password protection. Managing records of dates and times of password updates and tracking names of those responsible for managing these records enforces compliance.

When applied to logic structure, all executive leaders must be aware of the potential risk enveloped in accessing email files and managing how those files are retrieved, stored, and deleted, plays a role in how security is deployed across each executive leader's desk. Enforcing compliance with email security policy is mandatory! Noncompliance must be dealt with to minimize relaxing of commitment to adherence. Staying current with legal framework governing confidentiality and integrity of information assets belonging to the healthcare organization is priority. Insisting increased security of consumer information and avoid disseminating that information with third-party partners, must be prioritized, and assessed to ensure carelessness is absent and risk management is deployed. This includes staying compliant with local community health and safety requirements for the physical location of information assets. This also should include fire and safety hazard training and awareness.

The workflow of the system includes organization and business communication alliances that integrate usage of technology and information sharing to protect both sender and receiver from cyberattack victimization. Ensuring all network servers are backed up and archived daily. Making sure information systems are operating effectively and configured correctly is priority. No known vulnerabilities can exist in the information system workflow. Information assets must remain secured and no one without proper authority can have access to vital and trusted quality information belonging to the healthcare organization, including patents, intellectual property, consumer records, employee records, and insurance information for all employed or receiving services or products. Deployment of strategies that enhance security of these assets must be penetration tested to ensure security remains priority.

The next phases of penetration testing for healthcare and institutions of higher education will also differ. When deploying information gathering, focus must be on the specific type of information gathered, and designating who is responsible for gathering that information, and understanding how that gathered information will be stored and who this information should be shared with. This should include who must report how information is collected and stored and determine how it should be coded and logged for reference. Proper signatures must be affixed on all documents and time stamps must be added to allow ease of record retrieval when needed. This helps validate authenticity of information gathered. Next is vulnerability analysis, which was previously discussed. Doing so ensures consistency in activities relating to security strategies implemented at all levels of information gathering, storing, sharing, and receiving. Next is vulnerability analysis, which was previously discussed; this ensures consistency in activities relating to security strategies implemented at all levels of information gathering, storing, sharing, and receiving, are without vulnerabilities.

During the penetration testing phase there are several activities that must be considered. In-house testing involves managing pre-attack activity. Determining what method of attack will be used to gain access to the system and exploit vulnerabilities by cyberattackers is challenging. To overcome this challenge requires understanding how previous attack strategies were implemented by previous successful cyberattacks. In-house testing includes doing some research of previous attack methods used against competitors. If an organization has not experienced its initial attack, being aware of the type of attacks deployed against competitors helps. Too often, ransomware attacks and phishing attacks target institutions of higher education. Distributed denial of service attacks are commonly deployed against healthcare organizations. How do you prepare for an attack prior to it occurring? Training all personnel about both attack methods, including what to look for in an email message, and implementing penetration testing that test employees' responses, can benefit an organization tremendously. This can be as simple as sending an email to all personnel with the intent of assessing each personnel's timeline of discovering the intended test file. This helps determine who will report the file and determine which employee will defy their training and become victimized. This also involves implementing testing that assesses personnel's comprehension of the training they receive.

Penetration testing has six major components: network topology, network perimeter device, wireless device, web-based applications, commercial off-the-shelf testing, and in-house testing. Network topology testing includes baseline activity assessments, which are managed by intrusion detection and intrusion prevention software. AWS provides dynamic ID/IP software. In fact, AWS explains on its website that customers can conduct penetration testing on their AWS IP space or additional cloud providers for on-premises applications hosted by AWS or any third-party contracted testing. All security testing embodies Command and Control (C2), which requires prior approval. [11] AWS also explains that customers who discover any security issues with any of AWS services, during their security assessment, must contact AWS Security immediately to report the issue. However, AWS is explicitly adamant about some behavior during testing that is not permissible, including denial of service, distributed denial of service, simulated denial of service, simulated DDoS, and port flooding. Also prohibited is protocol flooding, domain name server hijacking via Route 53, and login request flooding.

Next step is firewall and VPN testing. This involves managing incoming and outgoing network traffic by assessing data packets and determining if the packet should be given authorization to enter the network. This requires establishing predetermined perimeter rule settings. The network's firewall creates a gateway between the internal network that is often trusted and the other network, i.e., the Internet, which should always be considered unsecure. Testing the firewall software should align with the manufacturer's recommendations and always be tested as such. Being aware of the known vulnerabilities within these applications is crucial to deterring successful cyberattacks from occurring. When it comes to VPN (virtual private network) healthcare organizations may not necessarily have their entire system connected. Ensuring all VPNs used on all network entrance points via web browsers and servers is another step to ensure concise security measures are implemented and operating as required. When these systems are neglected, it can wreak havoc on controlling system insecurities. Research conveys that there are two types of VPNs, i.e., SSL and IPsec. Port scanning and fingerprinting are two key methods in deploying a successful penetration test for these two VPNs. Research explains that port scanning enables the identification of an organization's VPN type. [12] In doing so, it is recommended to scan a particular range of IP addresses, instead of scanning the entire network. Using Zenmap as pointed out previously, helps assess what ports are open. If port number 500 is open, this is an IPSec VPN. If port number 443 is open, this is an SSL VPN. Staying knowledgeable of what ports are open helps lower the risks of these openings becoming threats to the security of the network. It is best to rely on password crackers to determine where vulnerabilities lie in passwords currently being used. It is also important to maintain written records of the activities deployed and how often these tests are run. Doing so helps to keep a managed record of penetration testing and helps to establish the baseline of activity that should be used to determine if a threat penetrated the system and how that threat is assessed, mitigated, and the system is backed up. This is a key requirement of network perimeter device assessment.

Wireless devices are also a target for attack. Research explains that wireless penetration testing encompasses six steps: reconnaissance, identifying wireless networks, vulnerability research, exploitation, reporting, and remediation. It is like the steps deployed across penetration testing methods for all system components. It is important to take the steps required and implement a system that will be adhered to throughout the lifecycle of the organization. Wireless reconnaissance requires implementing a war driving research method to determine the current list of Wi-Fi signals in the area. To achieve this, you need a laptop or mobile device, a vehicle to drive around the area in, a wireless network adaptor, and some packet capture analysis software. [13] All networks should be encrypted to prevent ease of access to the network. Scanning networks for vulnerabilities is next. Researching methods to achieving this goal is essential. Also, it is recommended to invest time learning how to implement the method and record strategies used to support your ongoing usage of this activity throughout the lifecycle of your role as information system or information technology practitioner with your organization.

Vulnerability research is important because it enables you to learn about vulnerabilities in systems and software your organization utilizes. One vulnerability your organization must be aware of and understand how to deter being victimized by is the four-way handshake. An encrypted key is shared across the Wi-Fi access point between the sender and receiver. A pre-key is generated to increase security of data encrypted. Typically, hackers sniff to determine if any weaknesses are present using a brute force attack. To deter this attack method, you need to understand why using a password cracker is helpful in determining if current passwords are secure. This is why utilizing the recommended length for a secure password must be adhered to. Research explains recommended length of a password is important because the longer the length of the password, the less likely it can be hacked. Organizations are required to rely and align their technology usage and information security with standardized federal regulated password length, which is outlined in the National Institute of Standards and Technology Special Publication 800-63-Digital Identity Guidelines. Although these guidelines are for federal agencies, these guidelines have become essential to support private sector entities. [14] This is why penetration testing is important.

During the exploitation of penetration testing, it is recommended to utilize the Airplay NG Suite tool. Using this tool enables de-authenticating a legitimate end user and enables capturing the initial four-way handshake. This also supports deployment of a dictionary attack. The purpose of this attack method is to leverage usage of an unauthorized Wi-Fi access point that is associated with the healthcare organization or institution of higher education. This aims to overpower a signal from a legitimate access point to force personnel to connect to the unauthorized access point. If an attacker is successful at gaining access, he/she will have full access over the flow of traffic utilizing the network. Therefore, reporting is essential. During the reporting step, it is invaluable to write down every action implemented and the actions and responses of everything that occurred. This should include gaining clarity regarding the required infrastructure and risk management system needed to support the scale of information assets the organization accumulates. When writing this report, research recommends including an executive summary detailing technical risks and any vulnerabilities discovered while deploying the process. Therefore, make sure all successful exploitations are recorded. This will help implement effective mitigation strategies.

Furthermore, an additional important component that needs auditing and assessments conducted regularly to ensure security is impenetrable is Web-based applications. Research explains there is no effective patching system for custom web applications. In fact, research studies report that web application flaws become entrance points for many breaches to occur and unauthorized intrusion incidents. [15] Adversaries focus their attention on these high-valued targets, directly abusing public-facing applications and targeting web apps as end users use them. Luckily for the inexperienced penetration tester, commercial off-the-shelf testing tools can also be beneficial. Keep in mind, understanding of these tools is crucial to determining their significance and benefit. Thus, it is important to research the drawbacks of using whatever testing tool, you rely on.

Auditing is instrumental in vulnerability assessment and penetration testing. The overall motive of an audit is to ensure that employees and managers are practicing policy requirements. This includes making sure employees and managers are efficiently, effectively, and economically utilizing and managing resources in compliance with the goals of their organization. This includes utilizing the Internet and disseminating email messages in compliance with applicable laws, regulations, policies, and procedures the organization must align with. Utilizing internal and external policy controls help prevent and deter usage errors and irregularities. The specific objective of auditing is to:

- verify both systems – internal and external control's implemented effectively and utilized with proper authorization.
- verify that policies are established, shared with all employees, and are being adhered to as well as to identify any abuse of such policies.
- verify that all employees and managers operate as required for their role and understand why the organization is implementing policies that govern the use of the Internet and dissemination of email messages across the organization's network.

4.10 Scope

The scope of the audit does not require an evaluation of internal and external control architecture of the organization's information system but is developed to evaluate and test compliance with the policies and procedures of internal and external control systems connected to technology. The audit should run for five to six months. It is the responsibility the CIO/CTO to establish and maintain a system of internal and external risk management controls to effectively comply with approved policy and procedures of the organization. One objective of internal and external risk management controls is to provide management assurance that all assets are safeguarded from loss or theft and unauthorized usage, and that all daily operations are executed in alignment with the management's authorization and effectively documented. The purpose of the audit report is to provide management objective analysis and recommendations concerning the activities reviewed. The audit report is an effective tool that helps management discern and implement improvements where necessary.

4.11 Audit Procedures

- Interview department personnel integral to the internal audit of all documents, all policies and procedures, to better comprehend current technologies used by the organization to evaluate and monitor email and Internet usage by employees and managers.
- Evaluate the organization's Internet and email server system risk management control, implement updated authorization access levels, establish the range of Internet usage employees are allocated.
- Select a sample of employee Internet usage history and email server history and content to create a baseline of usage auditing.
- Perform proper technology assessments to evaluate and test the organization's Internet and email security risk management controls against malware, virus protectors, and firewall intrusion to ensure these security controls are configured correctly and operating as needed.

Auditing the operating system enables you to understand how it is configured to operate in alignment with compliance requirements of Sarbanes Oxley Act of 2002. It is invaluable to provide managers assurance that the selected approved internal controls are in place and working effectively, and if problems are discovered, they will be addressed and corrected immediately! Reports will be developed and kept maintaining a written record of incidents, in the event the appropriate controls are not in place correctly. Otherwise, the integrity of the data and/or information generated from the system would be questionable for accuracy by internal and external auditors. Furthermore, the audit should verify systems and applications are appropriate to the users' needs, efficient, and adequately controlled to ensure validity, reliability, timeliness, and security of input, processes, and output at current and projected levels of system activity. [16] It is important to include the following steps to gather the necessary evidence to base the audit findings, conclusions, and recommendations. Gathering evidence, conduct inquiry; this can be achieved through interviews with end users and any IT support technician. Conduct an observation; this includes walking through the organization to become familiar with department procedures and assess all physical controls – information security. Next, you need to conduct an inventory, including physical examination of all goods and/or products on location. As well as conduct an analytical procedure. This is a review of data gathered from statistical or financial data on Excel spreadsheets or other data files. Last, you must conduct test procedures to ensure all data found on files is accurate and recorded in compliance with organizational policy and procedures.

To improve your understanding of an audit, embedded is a sample of an audit deployed on an organization's IT system. Reviewing the objective and comparing it with the objectives of your organization will improve how auditing is implemented to help decrease the number of successful cyberattack incidents deployed against your organization.

The objective of this IT strategy audit is to investigate the organization's current IT infrastructure. This audit focuses on IT performance of the following: alignment with organizational business strategies, IT organizational architecture, IT infrastructure, IT security, and IT project management. Adhering to this audit is to be beneficial because it shares the success rate of incidents deterred based on the number of decreased security and vulnerability flaws discovered.

4.12 Executive Summary

Your organization's IT department has attempted to implement the necessary steps to define IT strategies that align with the organization's strategy, especially since the organization is aware of the current IT infrastructure and organizational issues. For instance, laptops are often stolen from the office. Data files are not secured during transmission and at rest. There have been rumors that customer data and intellectual property has been lost or misplaced. This was when temporary staff was accessing the computer network and ineffectively securing files they accessed. Passwords were not being updated regularly and end users were not using recommended lengths. Although these issues have been noted, conducting this IT audit will enable IT managers and administrators to build on the current IT infrastructure and define strategies to help protect and secure these infrastructures from unauthorized access and unwanted attacks. The recommendations resulting from this audit include:

- *IT security* – the organization must establish a better security team, which comprises knowledgeable individuals from all departments, who can effectively monitor and manage the organization's security initiatives. This security team must be sanctioned to foster collaboratively and regularly across the organization. The organization needs to integrate system updates and patches as needed. It has been noted that Microsoft updates are conducted only once a month, and some updates are often missed. Also, third-party products such as Adobe Acrobat Reader are not being kept up to date regularly.

- *IT infrastructure* – the organization uses Microsoft servers and PCs with several Mac computers to perform design work. Personnel uses Active Directory, and a web server for their Internet website, which four servers are used as file sharing (one in each office), and four servers are hosting architecture applications. There is a training server, five MS SQL database servers, and two Microsoft Exchange servers for email. Each satellite office has three to four servers for storing files and running local applications. Each office has its own decentralized wireless network connected to the production network. Each employee has a desktop or laptop PC operating on Windows 10. HR personnel are using laptops for conducting interviews without secured virtual systems. Currently, the organization outsources their email spam filter and all HR applications to two separate third-party companies. HR applications should not be monitored by two separate third-party companies. This is a security risk.
- *IT architecture* – the organization should continue leveraging a matrix-organizational team to devise a set of architectural standards and policies that should encompass key elements, including processing platforms, database standards, consistent deployment of agreed technology stacks, and security standards.
- *IT project management* – the organization should continue all procedures that ensure alignment of IT projects to business sponsorship and prioritization. Doing so can result in optimized business benefits, solely derived from IT initiatives.

It is imperative to have a clearly conveyed overview of the organization. This should include details such as the number of employees working in office, the number of locations the business operates in, the number of employees at each location, as well as have a clear definition of the physical security of these locations. Physical security should encompass building perimeters, parking lot infrastructure, such as the number of entrance points, number of parking spaces available, number of external cameras on the external building and internal camera systems. How often these cameras are updated? How often are tapes retrieved and stored before being erased? These are some questions that should be asked when assessing physical security of a location. Are there cameras internally? How many? Where are they located? Who is controlling these systems? How often are these systems audited and replaced? What company is working in partnership with the organization to provide these services? A clear overview of your organization should be conveyed, such as it is sampled below:

The current IT management and administration operation for this organization should remain in place. However, integrating cloud computing can be beneficial in helping enhance security. Deploying an Enterprise Cloud User and Cisco AP 541N might be useful. Benefits of the Cisco AP 541N include robust wireless coverage and performance, advance clustering intelligence, highly secure guest access, strong security, deployment flexibility, scalable design, and an integrated solution. Cisco conveys that the Cisco AP 541N solution comes with three years of device-level service as an option. This includes telephone and online chat support through the Cisco Small Business Support Center, software updates and bug fixes, and access to the Cisco Small Business Support Community. If a wireless access point needs to be replaced, the service also includes next-business-day advance hardware replacement where services are available.

The technological infrastructure of this organization is complex. Major concerns include recent number of stolen laptop computers and data files not being secured during transmission and at rest. Although these issues have been noted, the organization's current IT infrastructure is not favorable to the rapid growth and organizational objectives of this organization. With this IT audit taking place, the organization must respectfully adhere to all recommendations and implement the necessary changes to spearhead the organization toward IT security compliance.

Next, is deployment of the risk assessment and recommendations to improve the risk discovered. Outlining the risk will increase knowledge sharing and help reduce risk that can result in vulnerabilities. Risk exists on outdated operating systems. Configuring operating systems for manufacturer's updates should be mandatory! Ensuring all servers are updated and configured correctly is also important. Ensuring that no default passwords are utilized to secure these tools is helpful in deterring a cyber incident. It is also important all software integrated on the devices are updated and configuration settings are set to secure applications from external tampering. When utilizing third-party software, it is essential that these applications are updated as well by the recommendation of the manufacturer. Neglecting to do so can create an ease of access to the organization's system. Reviews posted on the Common Exposure and Vulnerabilities website share current and past vulnerabilities reported on software applications. Learn more about this at the following link: https://cve.mitre.org/cgi-bin/cvekey.cgi?keyword=-Adobe+Acrobat+Reader+2024 [17].

Thus, developing and implementing policy that enforces compliance with risk assessment guidelines and procedures is important to controlling how personnel and executive leaders align their actions and activities in helping support the organization in protecting its usage of technology tools. Aligning organizational policy with recommendations and guidelines of the NIST SP 800 series is a key strategy in supporting the need of any organization when completing an IT strategy audit.

4.13 Summary

Usage of penetration testing was introduced by the U.S. Department of Defense and its Tiger team, which introduced the concept and practice of security testing. This concept and method of internally and externally targeting and attacking organization's hardware and software to locate and discover vulnerabilities, has grown to become a dynamic strategy in preparing for cyberattacks. This method of defense has helped many public and private sector entities increase their defense against cyberattacks. The number of healthcare organizations and institutions of higher education that are victimized by cyberattacks continues growing exponentially. This creates grave reason for consistent methods of penetration testing. Using the six methods of penetration testing, i.e., network topology, network perimeter device, wireless device, web-based applications, commercial off-the-shelf testing, and in-house testing, can play a significant role in supporting an organization in controlling the vulnerabilities woven in their system. Neglecting to implement penetration testing can hinder the ability to effectively safeguard an organization from cyberattack. Even though the usage of penetration testing is growing, healthcare organizations and institutions of higher education continue experiencing a rise in cyberattacks. Common attack methods include distributed denial of service attacks, ransomware, and other malware attacks. Staying current in trends of cyberattack methods will enable organizations to improve how they prepare for potential attacks. Staying current with software updates as recommended can also improve how vulnerabilities in software are managed. Neglecting to take action that prevents and deter cyberattacks is neglecting to implement effective cyber mitigation strategies to control the increase of budget spending. Unless personnel are trained to understand the risk associated with software applications usage, they will remain a risk factor. Adopting and adhering to recommendations and guidelines published by the U.S. National Institute of Standards and Technology and their NIST SP 800 series publications, is a best fit for both healthcare organizations and institutions of higher education.

4.14 Investigative Scenario

Bradley Healthcare Organization is a community-based healthcare clinic with approximately 50 employees operating in two regional areas. The main office is in San Diego, CA, which host 15 employees. The second office is in a suburb neighborhood where physical security has not been a concern.

Bradley Healthcare Organization current IT infrastructure embodies:

- Microsoft servers and laptops are used to perform daily work operations. Active Directory is utilized as well as four additional servers for file sharing. There are two servers housing medical file information and insurance information, and two Microsoft Exchange servers for email.
- There are two Windows 2008 servers in the main office, one is virtualized on one physical server.
- System updates and patches have not been conducted in six months. Third-party software applications such as Adobe Acrobat Reader and Chrome browser have missed updates over the last three months.
- Both offices operate their own decentralized wireless network connection and rely on default passwords that have not been updated since the initial installation.
- The network sits behind a gateway router and firewall. Commercial antivirus software is in use, but it is not automatically updated across the company. Some employees are working remotely and utilizing their login and password to gain access to the corporate system, which these passwords are not updated regularly. Temporary workers are often logging onto the system as well.

Some of the known issues with the IT infrastructure and organization include:

- Some laptops have been stolen out of the office in the last three months.
- Medical files are not kept secure, at rest or while in transit.
- Multi-factor authentication login details are often left on post-IT notes on some employee's desks.

As the cybersecurity leader for this organization, what is your first step in gaining control over the risks in these offices? How do you plan to implement a strategy that can update these offices on their negligence of cybersecurity and cyberattack mitigation? What policy must be developed and implemented to control this negligence? What type of training must be implemented to ensure this disorganization does not occur again? How can an audit help improve vulnerability assessment with this healthcare organization?

4.15 Discussion Questions

1. Who started penetration testing?
2. What is NIST SP 800-95 for?
3. What is NIST SP 800-12 Rev. 1 for?
4. What is NIST SP 800-53 Rev. 5 for?
5. Why is NIST SP 800-152 important?
6. What type of hacker possesses the knowledge of hacking and understands hacking tools that help discover weaknesses?
7. What is the objective of using the FAIR threat event frequency table?
8. What are the three audit tests to perform to determine if compliance with a policy in a department is adhered to?
9. When should the Sarbanes Oxley Act of 2002 be relied on?
10. What can hackers use to sniff out vulnerabilities on passwords?

Glossary

Black-hat hacker – considered the “bad guy” who targets system vulnerabilities to unleash malicious software that cripples a system for nefarious purposes.

Brute force attack – an aggressive attack with malicious intent to crack passwords, login authentication, and encryption keys to gain access to sensitive files for nefarious reasons, including to do costly damage.

CIA triad – confidentiality, integrity, and availability, standards enacted by the U.S. Department of Defense and NASA.

Continuous internal penetration testing – deployment of daily testing and assessment activities on the information system and information technology tools to ensure no vulnerabilities exist.

Dictionary attack – using a variation of words, numbers, and phrases to gain access to a system without authorization.

Ethical hacker – a contracted professional external hacker or internal professional hacker of an organization who deploys a legitimate hack attack on the network to test for insecure entrance points and system vulnerabilities.

Gray-hat hacker – self-proclaimed ethical hackers who focus on hacker tools with a child-like curiosity.

War driving – cruising in a vehicle searching for network vulnerabilities to gain access on a network without authorization for exploitation.

White-hat hacker – a professional hacker who used their skills to assess vulnerabilities on a network without nefarious purpose.

References

[1] Shari, Z., Aziz, A.S.E.M., Zolkefley, I.K., Sadjirin, R., & Raus, M.I.M. (2014, June 17). Implementing IT Security Penetration Testing in Higher Education. [PDF] Retrieved from: https://www.researchgate.net/publication/275338607_Implementing_IT_Security_Penetration_Testing_in_Higher_Education_Institute

[2] Whitman, E.M. & Mattord, J. H. (2017). Management of Information Security, (5th Ed). Cengage Learning. Boston, MA.

[3] Palatty, J. N. (2022, December 7). A Brief History of Penetration Testing. [Website] Retrieved from: https://www.getastra.com/blog/security-audit/history-penetration-testing/

[4] Alhammmadi, J.M. (n.d.). Continuous Internal Penetration Testing. [PDF] Retrieved from: https://www.researchgate.net/publication/371187537_Continuous_Internal_Penetration_Testing_CIPT

[5] Vinitha, K.P. (2016). International Journal of Engineering Research and Technology-Ethical Hacking. [PDF] Retrieved from: https://www.ijert.org/research/ethical-hacking-IJERTCONV4IS06008.pdf

[6] National Institute of Standards and Technology, (2012). Information Security. Retrieved from: https://csrc.nist.gov/publications/detail/sp/800-30/rev-1/final

[7] Wheeler, E. (2011). Security Risk Management: Building an Information Security Risk Management Program from the Ground Up. Syngress Elsevier, Waltham, MA

[8] Simpson, T.M. & Antill, N. (2017). Hands-On Ethical Hacking and Network Defense. (3rd Ed). Cengage Learning. Boston, MA.

[9] Wireshark, (2024). Download Wireshark. [Website] Retrieved from: https://www.wireshark.org/about.html

[10] Wireshark, (2024). Wireshark University. [Website] Retrieved from: https://www.wireshark.org/learn

[11] Amazon Web Services, (2024). Penetration Testing. [Website] Retrieved from: https://aws.amazon.com/security/penetration-testing/

[12] Breach Lock, (2021, March 11). VPN Penetration Testing Explained. [Website] Retrieved from: https://www.breachlock.com/resources/blog/vpn-penetration-testing-explained/

[13] Stankovic, S. (2023, March 18). How to Perform a Wireless Penetration Test. [Website] Retrieved from: https://purplesec.us/perform-wireless-penetration-test/#Reconnaissance

[14] Poza, D. (2021, January 22). NIST Password Guidelines and Best Practices for 2020. [Website] Retrieved from: https://auth0.com/blog/dont-pass-on-the-new-nist-password-guidelines/

[15] Conrad, E., Zdrnja, B. & McKenzie, T. (2024). SEC542: Web App Penetration Testing and Ethical Hacking. [Website] Retrieved from: https://www.sans.org/cyber-security-courses/web-app-penetration-testing-ethical-hacking/

[16] Davis, A., Gallegos, F., & Senft, S. (2013). Information Technology Control and Audit. (4th Ed). CRC Press Taylor & Francis Group. Boca Raton, FL., p. 88

[17] Common Vulnerabilities and Exposures, (2024). Adobe Acrobat Reader. [Website] Retrieved from: https://cve.mitre.org/cgi-bin/cvekey.cgi?keyword=Adobe+Acrobat+Reader+2024

5

Cybersecurity Forensics Tools and Usage Techniques

Learning Objectives

- Assess computer forensics tools and applications for cybersecurity leadership.
- Investigate email and social media forensics tools.
- Distinguish big data analytics forensics for healthcare organizations and institutions of higher education.

5.1 Introduction

The most dynamic method of investigating a cyberattack incident deployed with a computer device is using computer forensics tools and methodologies. Computer forensics investigation includes research and incident response. [1] Since the inception of digital forensics, the growth and usage of computer forensics has impacted the public and private sector, domestically and internationally. The enactment of federal and international laws and policy encompassing privacy rights, issues of ethics, and integrity has evolved exponentially. And while the number of cybercrimes solved using computer forensics tools and applications has helped pique the interest of private sector entities, hoping to reduce the threat of cybercrime impacting business and revenue earnings. Usage and reliance on computer forensics tools continue growing, and so have the skills and capabilities of cybercriminals, who, too, understand how to optimize computer forensics tools and artificial intelligence to gain access to targeted computers and networks. To improve how you outthink cybercriminals requires more than a PhD. It requires having access to a plethora of information on the right computer forensics tools; knowing how to utilize each tool, and why each tool is used and beneficial. It is essential to understand how to effectively deploy a computer forensics investigation. This requires understanding what should be assessed during the investigation; what should be collected, and how to securely store the collected evidence to ensure safe and thorough usage of collected evidence can be utilized to solve the case and bring the culprit to justice. Furthermore, there is a need to understand what laws protect the rights of private and public sector entities and how those laws impact the ability to deploy a secure and effective computer forensics investigation. This chapter will help answer some of your concerns about computer forensics investigation tools, and discuss Snort and Wireshark, two useful computer forensics tools, you can use with cyberattack incident investigation. This chapter will enable you to improve how you assess computer forensics tools and applications for cybersecurity leadership. This chapter will also provide details about big data analytics and how artificial intelligence and machine learning can help control risk management factors for healthcare organizations and institutions of higher education. A summary reiterates these findings, and an investigative scenario helps you begin walking a mile in an investigator's shoes. Discussion questions help you reassess what you learned throughout this chapter.

In 2006, the United States National Institute of Standards and Technology published a profound publication titled *Guide to Integrating Forensic Techniques into Incident Response*, under special series publication 800-86. The abstract conveys the intent of this publication is to support organizations in investigating computer security incidents and troubleshooting minor information technology problems during the deployment of performing a computer and network forensic investigation. [2] Since the publication of this document, efforts have increased to provide effective methods of collecting computer forensics. In 2016, computer forensics became known as digital forensics. Most experts in the field of digital forensics are self-taught. [3] The type of computer crimes commonly investigated using digital forensics, include company policy violations, embezzlement, email harassment, murder, leaks of proprietary information, and terrorism. Law enforcement, attorneys, network administrators, and private investigators rely on digital forensics experts to effectively investigate computer crimes and collect evidence in support of criminal and civil investigations. Digital forensics is a scientific method of investigating, collecting, examining, and analyzing information and preserving that information with integrity, so the information remains intact while in transmission from and to the location of the official investigation. Digital forensics is collected from hard drives, computer device storage, and software application files. External hard drives and USB port drives are common tools data and information files are stored in. Please be aware that gaining access to information from any computer device or technology tool within a company can only be done when the owner or founder of the company gives their permission to extract such information.

Network forensics analysis relies on log files to determine when a device user last accessed the device and to determine the previous URL addresses viewed. Too often, computer device end users utilize a browser that tracks their web search history making it easy to follow up behind them. Most browsers collect details about website addresses, including URL, date of the last visit, and sometimes, the time stamp is provided. This information is vital in many digital forensics investigations because it enables the network forensic investigator to assess patterns of web browsing activity as it correlates with the individual's habits of Internet browsing engagement.

Unlike data recovery, which encapsulates retrieving information previously deleted by mistake or lost during a reboot of the computer system digital forensics recovers data that was intentionally hidden or deleted, to ensure this information is retrievable and useful for an investigation. Evidence retrieved is considered inculpatory, which means incriminating. Evidence can also be exculpatory, which means it is used to clear a suspect. When deploying a digital forensics investigation, digital forensics tools have become helpful in determining what evidence is available on a computer or mobile device, and enable digital forensics investigators to assess the value of such evidence collected. There are several software application tools available for digital forensics investigations. Some of these software applications can be downloaded for free. Downloading these software applications is easy. Knowing how to utilize them correctly is challenging. The list of software applications discussed in this chapter was discovered on the University of San Diego | Online Blog authored by Michelle Moore, PhD., titled *23 Best Network Forensic Tools and Software.* [4] To help you determine what forensics software tool will best serve your digital forensics investigational needs, two software applications are outlined below: Snort and Wireshark.

5.2 Snort

Snort is an open-source computer forensics software application often used for intrusion Prevention. Effective utilization of Snort requires knowledge of Snort rules, which enable end users to define malicious network activity through Snort rules. Snort can be utilized for packet sniffing or network intrusion prevention. Snort can be utilized for business or personal computer devices. Snort rules are provided in two formats. The first format is community ruleset. The second format is Snort subscriber ruleset. [5]

Snort rules are downloadable and can be installed easy. Once the source code is installed on the device, you will receive a unique identifier which is required to access your Snort instance. This retrieves your Snort ruleset. All end users have access to the registered rule set. Snort provides a video tutorial to support end users during Step 3 of the installation process. It is highly recommended to utilize this tutorial to help you understand the challenges that embody usage of this application. Snort has been downloaded 5 million times and has over 600,000 registered end user accounts. You can utilize Snort with a subscription model, which provides a personal usage application; this cost $29.00 for a one-year subscription. With that subscription, you gain Snort ruleset, typically before nonsubscription end users. You also receive advance details of exploits and the ability to submit false positive/negative reports. This subscription model is useful for home network environment or educational purposes. The business subscription model is $300.00. This package includes priority response to false positives/negatives and rulesets. However, this subscription does not support license to redistribute Snort subscriber ruleset. The integrator package is designed for those interested in integrating Snort into their individual application or server for commercial resale.

To enhance the learning capabilities of end users, Snort delivers online instruction courses as well as on-demand and onsite training. Developed by Cisco, learners who hold a System Security Certified Practitioner, or are Certified Information Systems Security Professionals can acquire continued education credits for every hour of training they complete. This credit can be acquired through virtual courses. Simply provide your certification number during registration and you will receive those credits. To learn more about this virtual training courses log on to http://www.cisco.com/web/learning/learning_services/courses/security.html Clicking register now enables you to view the various time zones. Usage of a credit card is required to make payment. Learners must be 21+ to register for these courses.

Downloading Snort can be complicated if you are unaware of the application you need to install. On the website, there are three source applications: snort3-3.1.7.8.0.tar.gz, snort3_extra-3.1.7.8.0.tar.gz, and libdaq-3.0.1.4.tar.gz. Using the free download, you want to click and install the first file listed. Be sure to download all documentation files, including snort_user.pdf, snort_upgrade.pdf, and snort_reference.pdf. Using the PDF files are beneficial because it enables you to read the instructions thoroughly. Neglecting to read the instructions will impede your ability to write your code requirements needed to successfully deploy the software application. Snort PDF User Manuals are often 116 pages or more. Read the manual. The recently published edition of Snort manual is dated January 16, 2024. This manual provides a step-by-step guide to help you configure command lines, files, and rules. You also learn about concepts, including terminology, modules, parameters, plugins, operation processing, rules, and pattern matching. Keep in mind, Snort rules are required throughout the entire time, you are working with this application. The reference manual is essential because it provides the list of codes one will need to apply when configuring Snort rules for usage. Please pay close attention to the intrusion prevention codes. This will ensure your application configuration settings are correct and will operate as needed. This manual is 265 pages. Thus, take your time and read what is needed throughout this document to support your usage of this application. I cannot stress this enough!

It is recommended to access the provided resources, including watching the videos provided. Doing so will help reduce your stress and concerns of working with this application, especially if it is your first time. You may need to brush up on your coding skills because the complexity level is not for a beginner. Writing rules throughout your application configuration will determine the success of your usage of this application. Thus, read the white papers provided and review all multi-media How-To's. If you run into configuration problems, you can certainly reach out for support accessing the "Contact" page on the website.

Primary modes of Snort include sniffer mode, logging mode, and network intrusion detection Mode. Understanding each mode and how to configure rules is invaluable. Therefore, deploying research is recommended for successful usage of this software tool. When defining Snort rules, you need to define the protocol, this can be either TCMP, TCP, UDP or additional protocols. [6] Next, you need to determine the direction; matching traffic from a server to the client or matching a client to a server. The code for this direction is "<- "or ">- " You will also need to determine the source and destination IP address and ports, before defining the rule options. Rule options include content, threshold, PCRE, and class type. Additionally, you will need to understand Snort rule headers; this includes rule actions, protocol, source IP addresses, and destination IP addresses. The source port and destination port and direction are required. There are many cheat sheets available online. Cyvatar provided a cheat sheet on its website in January 2022. You can access that at https://cyvatar.ai/write-configure-snort-rules/ [7].

5.3 Wireshark

Like Snort, Wireshark is a free open-source application that can be downloaded and utilized for network protocol analysis. You can access Wireshark at https://wireshark.org Wireshark can be used on Windows and Mac operating systems. When installing this software for Windows, you want to install Windows x64 Installer. It is suggested to verify downloads using file hashing to determine the current release. On the website, you can locate the Signature ID key file number. Wireshark can be accessed via third-party packages, including Alpine Linux, Apple/MacOS, Canonical/Ubuntu, and Oracle/Solaris 11. [8]

Wireshark is considered the world's most utilized and accessed network protocol analyzer. Using Wireshark enables you to inspect hundreds of protocols and deploy live captures and offline analysis. This application can capture network data via a GUI, or through a TTY-mode T-Shark utility. This tool can be used for VoIP analysis, and to read/write and capture various file types, including tcpdump, Pcap, Microsoft Network Monitor, Network Sniffing, NetScreen snooping, and WAN/LAN analyzing. This application renders decryption support for various protocols, including IPSec, Kerberos, SSL/TLS, and WPA/WPA2.

Unlike Snort, configuration is simple. Once you install the application, you can begin implementing your steps to retrieve the information you are seeking to acquire. As you click through the installation, be sure to create a shortcut for your desktop and click the Associate File extensions. You also want to set the installation for NpCap 1.78. You also will have the option to deploy a USB Capture. If you want that data from the device(s) you are installing the software on, you can configure that as well. Installation does not take much time. You also will be given the opportunity to configure the software to Restrict Npcap driver's access to Administrator only, support raw 802.11 traffic (and monitor mode) for wireless adapters and install Npcap in WinPcap API-compatible mode. Once the installation is complete and you click the desktop icon, you will see the following screen, showing the Adapter for loopback traffic capture as conveyed in Figure 5.1 below:

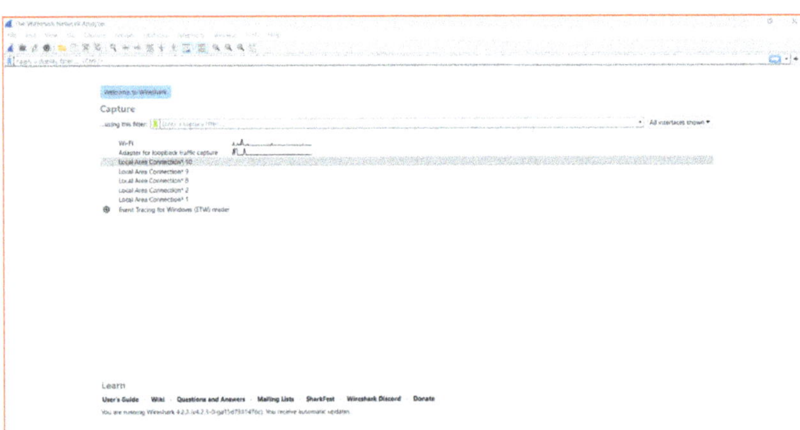

Figure 5.1 Wireshark network analyzer.

You can also deploy a Capture filter, which displays the Ethernet address, Ethernet type, IPv4 address, IPv6 address, TCP only, HTTP TCP port (80), and non-HTTP and non-SMTP to/from www.wireshark.org, as shown in Figure 5.2 below:

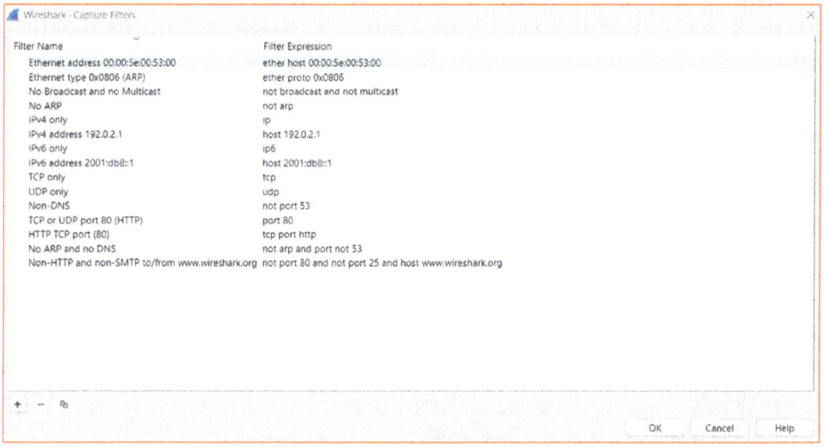

Figure 5.2 Wireshark capture filters.

When you click on Capture File Properties, you can access the Local Area Connection, which provides details of the download file name, Hash (SHA 256), Hash (SHA1), Format, Encapsulation and the Capture type – i.e., Hardware, OS, or Application. You also gain access to the Interfaces and Statistics. When deploying a new Capture, simply click the tab and click "Options." A screen will appear with three tabs, i.e., Input, Output, and Options. On the Input screen, you will have a list of Interfaces and a visual of the Traffic, link-layer headers, Snaplen (B), Buffer (MB), Monitor, and Capture Filter as shown in Figure5.3 below:

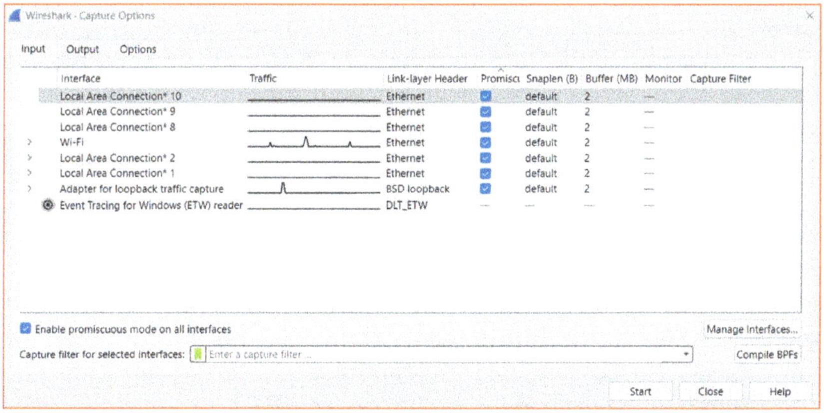

Figure 5.3 Wireshark capture options.

As you view this window, you will see the Traffic analyzer pulse connecting to the Ethernet and the Snaplen (b) will be set in default. The Buffer (MB) will be set in 2. Now click the Output tab and enter the File name, by clicking the Browse tab, which will enable you to see the list of Documents. Selecting a file will place the file name in the File list. Now, click the "Output format" (pcapng) and click "Create a new file automatically." You will be able to configure the packets and set the kilobytes, seconds, and hours. The compression will automatically be set to None. The ringer buffer will be set automatically for two files. You can configure this as you desire. Next, click the Options tab. You will see that the Display Options are preset for Update list of packets in real-time and automatically scroll during live capture. The Name Resolution will be preset for MAC addresses. The preset will be configured for the Stop capture automatically after the number of packets, files, and seconds are configured. You can update these settings as you need. Now, click the Start button. Be sure to configure the settings correctly. You will receive notifications informing you if there are incorrect configurations. Once you click the Start button, the analyzer will show the Wi-Fi traffic flow, and the Adapter for Loopback traffic capture.

Research explains that Wireshark provides the ability to examine live network traffic. [9] Research also explains that Wireshark enables administrators to examine data previously captured. Wireshark provides language filters and TCP session reconstruction utility. This means that Wireshark's TCP tracks the position of all TCP sessions and renders information regarding problems or potential issues that have been detected. An analysis is deployed after each TCP packet, once a capture file is opened. Packets are processed in chronological order as they appear in the packet list, enabling administrators to disable this component using the Analyze TCP sequence numbers and TCP dissector preference. [10] Overall, Wireshark has a dynamic scalability for packet sniffing and can be used across various languages.

As you learned, understanding the scale of computer forensics tools and applications for cybersecurity leadership is invaluable. When working with Windows, Linux, or Macintosh file systems, there may be some incompatibility with the software applications relied on from one operating system to another. Windows is the most utilized operating system worldwide, accounting for 68.15% usage of desktop, tablets, and console in operating system markets since, February 2024. [11] When determining how data is stored on a disk, the file system becomes the road map to data storage. Accessing a computer to retrieve data files requires understanding the operating system so you can easily access that system and modify system settings as needed. So, understanding the basic input/output system (BIOS) can help reduce your stress of trying to determine how to access and retrieve data stored on the file system. Therefore, you must be familiar with disk drives and how data is organized on a disk, so you can locate it correctly. The components of a disk drive include geometry, which refers to disk logical structure of platters, tracks, and sectors. [12] The head is the device that assesses and writes data to a drive. Tracks are concentric circles on a disk platter, which data is typically found. Cylinders are columns of tracks on several disk platters. However, platters have two surfaces: top and bottom. Sectors are sections on a track comprised of 512 bytes.

Research explains that flash memory storage devices utilized in USB drives, laptops, tablets, and cell phones can be difficult for digital forensics examiners. If data deleted is not recoverable immediately that data might be lost forever. Flash memory has wear leveling. Once data is deleted on a hard drive, only references to this deleted data are removed, leaving the original data in an unallocated disk space. Using forensics recovery tools, data is recovered from magnetic media easily because experts can retrieve the unallocated space. However, retrieving data from USB drives is different because memory cells shift the data at the physical layer to additional cells with less reads and writes consistently. In fact, research reports that when dealing with solid-state devices, making a full forensic copy immediately is crucial, especially if you need to recover data from an unallocated disk space.

Keep in mind that laws differ from country to country. Depending on the jurisdiction and the laws regarding search and seizure, there may be limitations on how you acquire access and retrieve or utilize the data files discovered. In Microsoft file structures, sectors are paired in clusters. Clusters are storage allocation units for various sectors. They range from 512 bytes to 32,000 bytes. Pairing sectors reduces the overhead of writing or reading files to a disk. Windows OS groups several sectors into clusters. Clusters are numbered sequentially. The first sector of all disks embodies system areas, including the boot record and file structure database. Clusters and their logical and physical addresses are specific and easily become disk partitions. Windows OS may have three primary partitions on a logical drive. If someone desires to hide data on a hard disk, they can create hidden partitions using large unused space between each partition on a disk drive. However, you can examine a partition's physical layer using a disk editor, such as WinHex or Hex Workshop.

WinHex is a dynamic universal hexadecimal editor commonly used for computer forensics, data recovery, low-level data processing, and IT security. This tool can support inspection and editing of all types of files, recover deleted files or lost data from hard drives with corrupt file systems and from digital camera cards. Installation of WinHex is simple because this application is an open-source now available at https://www.x-ways.net/winhex/.

\WinHex features include disk editor for hard disks, floppy disks, CD-ROM and DVD, Zip files, Smart Media, and Compact Flash. There is a built-in interpretation of RAID systems and dynamic disks. The RAM editor enables access to physical RAM and addition processes' virtual memory data interpreter for 20 data types. WinHex supports erasing of confidential files, hard drive cleansing to protect privacy, and converts between binary, hex, and ASCII hex values. This application is easy to use and understand. Taking time to review this tool and its purposes can be instrumental in deploying an effective computer forensics investigation. One important aspect of WinHex is that it enables you to see file headers and additional critical components of a file. WinHex also helps you indicate the file system, determine a .bmp file type, and determine if a file is a Microsoft office file. [13]

Linux and Macintosh file systems differ greatly from Windows. Linux kernel is packaged with additional software applications, including GUI. This helps end users avoid needing to combine different open-source applications to design their work environment. Kernel aligns with Linux because Linux is the core of the Operating System (OS). [14] Top level directories of a Linux system, includes /usr, /etc, /home, /root, /dev, and /var. The /usr applies to various applications and commands and stands for binary, containing binary files utilized during the boot session. /etc embodies system configuration files. /home correlates for all end users and is found after their username. /root is a component of the home directory and is separate from other home directories. /dev is for device files which act as stand-ins, usually located on the main hard drive. And /var represents subdirectories, which stores email accounts.

Linux commands are case sensitive. Inputting the wrong capitalization means your command will be rejected and interpreted incorrectly. Linux commands rely on options to design variations of a command. Linux supports a wide scope of file types. Linux considers disk drives, monitors, tape drives, network interface cards, system memory, and directories as files. Linux has four parts that define the file system, including boot block, superblock, inode block, and data block. The boot block encompasses boot strap code that are instructions for startup. A Linux computer has one boot block. The superblock possesses vital information regarding the system and is a component of the metadata. This specifies disk geometry and the allocated space available as well as maintains track of all inodes. This also manages the file system and configuration information. Various copies of superblock are kept in various departments on a disk to support loss of vital data. Inode blocks are the first data after superblock. An inode is given to every file. A link is placed between inodes with known files and directories, so accessibility is easy. Data block is when directories and files are stored on disk drives.

Macintosh file structures are different. First, Mac files have two parts: data fork, where data is stored, and resource fork, where file metadata and application information are stored. Each of these forks embody essential information, such as resource map, resource header information for each file, windows locations as well as icons. Data fork embodies data the user creates, i.e., text or spreadsheets. Windows Word docx or Excel can also be read and write to data fork. Volume is used to store files. Macintosh forensics procedures require you to know where file system components are resting as well as know how these files are stored. For instance, Mac File Vault encrypts the entire disk with 128-bit encryption. Albeit this is outdated new recommendations for encryption is 256-bit encryption. [15] Additional encryption information you will discover is password details. Keychains are used to manage passwords. It is easy to locate keychain files that help show application and file passwords. In MacOS, deleted files are in the Trash Bin. There are several vendors that provide examining software for Mac OS file system, including ProDiscover Forensic Edition and Sleuth Kit. [16] Furthermore, Mac Acquisition processing requires making a disk image. You will need a Mac-compatible forensic boot CD/DVD to make an image. You will also need to write that image to an external drive, such as a USB drive. Once you acquire an acquisition, you will need to examine the file system using a forensics tool. Two recommended tools include X-Ways Forensics and AccessData FTK.

This brings us to a complex area of forensics because there are numerous forensics tools to utilize. First, there are hardware forensics tools that range from simple to single purpose to entire computer systems and servers. One dynamic workstation commonly relied on is FRED forensic workstation. FRED systems are great for forensics acquisition and analysis workstations. [17] There are also software forensics tools grouped into command-line applications and GUI. Software forensics tools are used to copy data from a suspect's device to an image file. GUI applications can acquire all structures in an image file. And there are digital forensics tools that help with acquisition, validation and verification, extraction, reconstruction, and reporting [18]. During acquisition subfunctions include:

- Physical data copy
- Logical data copy
- Data acquisition format

- Command-line acquisition
- GUI acquisition
- Remote, live, and memory acquisition

Disk acquisition formats differ from raw data to vendor-specific proprietary. Validation and verification partners collectively. Validation confirms that the forensics tool is operating as expected. Verification renders two sets of data identification via calculating hash values and using another type of method. Filtering becomes instrumental because it enables sorting and separating good data from bad data. All forensics tools provide methods of verification that compare original drives with images. Using the National Software Reference Library can be useful in determining what forensics software tools best serve the needs of your investigation. You can locate that library reference at https://www.nist.gov/itl/ssd/software-quality-group/national-software-reference-library-nsrl

Extraction is a recovery task deployed during digital investigation, but it is challenging to master. During an extraction, the following subfunctions are relied on:

- Data viewing
- Keyword searching
- Decompressing or uncompressing
- Carving
- Decrypting
- Bookmarking or tagging

Digital forensics tools provide data-viewing mechanisms for understanding digital evidence, including logical drive structures such as folders and files. Digital forensics involves reconstructing fragments of files that were deleted. This is called "carving" in North America. In Europe it is called "salvaging." When an investigation encounters compression or Zip files – i.e., WinZip, the correct algorithm is applied to uncompress files. However, a major issue in digital investigations involves analyzing, recovering, and decrypting data. Files, disk drives, and disk partitions can be encrypted. These types of files can be problematic during an investigation. Thus, using OS Forensics V-11 is the "go-to" for support. You can access that forensics tool at https://www.osforensics.com/

Compiled is a list of computer forensics tools, you can take your time to review to better understand and determine which one of these tools will be instrumental in supporting your investigation needs. Tools on this list may not be available for use in your country. Please be sure to investigate your country's laws and policy regarding usage of computer forensics tools and data acquisition for search and seizure.

5.4 Types of Digital Forensics Tools

- 7-Zip: http://www.7-zip.org/
- Kali Linux: https://www.kali.org/
- Oracle VirtualBox: https://www.virtualbox.org/
- MD5 & SHA Checksum Utility 2.0: https://raylin.wordpress.com/2013/06/04/md5-sha-checksum-utility-2-0/
- MD5Deep & HashDeep: http://md5deep.sourceforge.net/
- Windows SysInternals Suite: https://technet.microsoft.com/en-us/sysinternals/bb842062.aspx
    - Autoruns
    - Process Explorer
    - Process Monitor
    - TCPView
- FTK Imager: http://accessdata.com/product-download
    - Version3.4.2:http://accessdata.com/product-download/digital-forensics/ftk-imager-version-3.4.2
- Chrysocome: http://www.chrysocome.net/
    - Download page: http://www.chrysocome.net/download
    - dd for Windows: http://www.chrysocome.net/dd
- NetCat – available with nmap: https://nmap.org/ncat/
- The Sleuth Kit: http://www.sleuthkit.org/
    - Sleuth Kit Download: http://www.sleuthkit.org/sleuthkit/download.php
    - Autopsy: http://www.sleuthkit.org/autopsy/

  - NOTE: Both send to SourceForge for the download. Use the mirror if the main site doesn't work.

- OS Forensics (PassMark Software): http://www.osforensics.com/
  - Tools (OSFMount, OSFClone, etc): http://www.osforensics.com/tools/
- MiTeC Windows Registry Recovery: http://www.mitec.cz/wrr.html
- MiTeC Windows File Analyzer: http://www.mitec.cz/wfa.html
- RegRipper: https://github.com/keydet89/
- HashCalc: http://www.slavasoft.com/hashcalc/
- HashMyFiles: http://www.nirsoft.net/utils/hash_my_files.html
- WinHex: http://www.x-ways.net/winhex/
- NirSoft Web Browser Tools: http://www.nirsoft.net/web_browser_tools.html
- NirSoft WinPrefetchView: http://www.nirsoft.net/utils/win_prefetch_view.html
- JumpLister: http://www.woanware.co.uk/forensics/jumplister.html
- AstroGrep: http://astrogrep.sourceforge.net/
- Carver Recovery: https://code.google.com/p/carver-recovery/
- Bulk Extractor: http://www.forensicswiki.org/wiki/Bulk_extractor
- Memoryze (FireEye): https://www.fireeye.com/services/freeware/memoryze.html
- Volatility: http://www.volatilityfoundation.org/
- pList Editor Pro: http://www.icopybot.com/plist-editor.htm
- VirusTotal: https://www.virustotal.com/

5.5 Windows Tools

- Bleeping Computer Tutorials: http://www.bleepingcomputer.com/tutorials/have-i-been-hacked/
- Windows God Mode: http://www.bleepingcomputer.com/tutorials/enable-godmode-in-windows/

- Show-hidden: http://www.bleepingcomputer.com/download/show-hidden/
- RegShot (Windows Registry comparison): http://sourceforge.net/projects/regshot/
- RegAlyzer (browse & change the registry): https://www.safer-networking.org/products/regalyzer/
- FileAlyzer: https://www.safer-networking.org/products/filealyzer/
- Sandboxie: http://www.sandboxie.com/

5.6 Linux Tools

- 50 UNIX/Linux Sysadmin Tutorials: http://www.thegeekstuff.com/2010/12/50-unix-linux-sysadmin-tutorials/
- 20 Linux System Monitoring Tools: http://www.cyberciti.biz/tips/top-linux-monitoring-tools.html
- Linux Shell Scripting Tutorial (LSST) v2.0: http://bash.cyberciti.biz/guide/Main_Page
- Learning the Shell: http://linuxcommand.org/lc3_learning_the_shell.php
- Unix/Linux Command Reference: http://files.fosswire.com/2007/08/fwunixref.pdf
- Ubuntu reference: http://files.fosswire.com/2008/04/ubunturef.pdf
- Ubuntu cheat sheet: http://mhvlug.org/sites/default/files/Advanced_ubuntu_sheet.pdf

5.7 Malware Analysis Tools

- Windows SysInternals Suite: https://technet.microsoft.com/en-us/sysinternals/bb842062.aspx
    - Autoruns
    - Process Explorer
    - Process Monitor
    - TCPView
- Process Hacker: http://processhacker.sourceforge.net/

- Buster Sandbox Analyzer: (also a list of malware analysis services) http://bsa.isoftware.nl/
- Cuckoo Sandbox: http://www.cuckoosandbox.org/
- Lenny Zeltser:
- Free Toolkits for Automating Malware Analysis: https://zeltser.com/malware-analysis-tool-frameworks/
- Free automated malware analysis services: https://zeltser.com/automated-malware-analysis/

5.8 Email and Social Media Investigation

Email and social media networks are favorite spots for cybercriminals to catch personnel sleeping so they can integrate their cunning crafty schemes. One common attack methods personnel often become victimized by is phishing emails. A phishing message tries to lure the recipient to divulge sensitive information using false promises. Sometimes, these emails can embody signatures that mirror an authority that the recipient is familiar with, and the cybercriminal gains the details and information sought. Pharming is utilized when an email recipient is pointed to a fake website address. Because personnel are limited in knowledge regarding what to examine to determine if the email received is part of a pharming scheme, having clarity on the role of email in investigations is essential to improve training for personnel. Email messages are provided through the Internet and intranet. An intranet email system is utilized by private entities, while the Internet is used by public entities and individuals. On the intranet, the email server is a part of the local network, which is managed by the administrator. Google, Hotmail, and Yahoo email accounts, and those alike, are public email accounts. These service providers provide servers and administrators. When investigating intranet email, it is easy. But tracking public Internet email is hard. When investigating an email relating to a cybercrime, it is important to understand the Electronic Communications Privacy Act and the Stored Communications Act.

In the United States and some parts of Europe, these policies are adhered to and respected. Thus, violating these Acts can lead to civil infraction and costly liabilities. Before starting an email investigation, it is recommended to copy the email. You are also recommended to forward a copy of the email to another email address. Once you copy an email, look for the email header.

Copy and paste the email header onto a Word.docx document so you will be able to read the text using Windows Notepad, Linux Vim, or Apple TextEdit. If using Outlook, the instructions are as followed:

- Open Outlook and select the message you copied.
- Double click on the message and click File, Properties. If you review the Properties Internet header near the bottom of the frame, you will find the message header details.
- Select the message header text and press Ctrl+C to copy this message to the clipboard.
- Start Notepad and press Ctrl+V to paste the message header text. Save the document and close Outlook.

The main source of details you seek to assess is the email IP address, which provides the origin of the sender. You also want to examine the date and time stamp. File names of each attachment as well as any other unique message numbers are essential. Tracing an email message also helps determine the origin of the email. Using registry sites to learn details that are not available can be helpful. Websites such as the American Registry for Internet Numbers help map out an IP address and locate the domain's point of contact (www.arin.net). Also, http://www.internic.com/ is another web address where you can gain information regarding Information Domains Registration services. Using an email log is helpful in determining if an email is processed through a firewall. Firewalls manage log files which track Internet traffic destinations for networks. When a network administrator shared network firewall log files, these files can be opened using a text editor, such as Notepad. Research explains that some email service providers do not keep email logs for more than 30 days. Some keep these logs for less time. Email servers maintain copies of client's email, even after end users delete email messages from their inbox. Sometimes, these service providers may not delete deleted emails until the system is backed up. System administrators can retrieve deleted emails without restoring the entire email server.

Common forensics tools used for email investigation include:

- Data Numen recovers email, back-up and archive files, and database, images, and documents. Learn more at https://www.datanumen.com/
- Paraben E-mail Examiner recovers email from various service providers. Learn more at https://paraben.com/free-digital-investigation-software/

- Exterro FTK Imager creates forensics images, preview data, and enable evaluation of digital evidence. Learn more at https://www.exterro.com/digital-forensics-software/ftk-imager

Social media investigation can be challenging. However, gaining access to evidence from social media, includes evidence regarding cyberbullying and witness tampering; helps determine if intellectual property has been violated and conveys, who posted what and when. Using big data analytics is useful to compile data from various environments, including YouTube, Facebook, Instagram, X, and other mediums. After all, the types of files you will be extracting include image files, mp4 files, .jpg, .png, and bitmap files. These files can vary in size and contain detailed information, which is helpful during an investigation. Web crawling software for forensics can be helpful in supporting social media investigations. A current list of forensics tools utilized for social media investigation can be found at the Afentis Forensics Group. Learn more about this group at https://www.afentis.com/. Also, Oxygen Forensics provides analysis for Facebook account data. This enables investigators to acquire details about chats, contacts, and feeds. Files are supported in various languages, including English, German, French, Spanish, and Italian. [19] To learn more, log on to https://oxygenforensics.com/en/resources/facebook-account-data-import/.

5.8.1 Big data analytics as a forensics tool

Research explains that big data analytics in healthcare plays a significant role in helping administrative, business, and clinical areas. Big data analytics can be compiled from databases, transaction data, unstructured content of emails and documents, data from devices, and sensors. [20] Research also explains that decisions made in medical facilities are data driven. Usage of big data analytics enables healthcare organizations to predict the future. This also enables the ability to understand trends regarding issues relating to the past. Big data analytics enables healthcare organizations to analyze large datasets of their patients and identify clusters and correlations aligning between datasets that can help create predictive models reliant on data mining techniques. Research explains that healthcare organizations need to effectively implement security measures and methodologies to increase protection of their big data. This includes securing hardware and software as well as clinical and administrative information from both internal and external risks. Using a four-phase big data lifecycle model – data collection, data storage, data processing and analysis, and knowledge creation – can be instrumental in supporting healthcare organizations in securing big data, including patient's privacy. This approach enables healthcare cybersecurity leaders to define a coding system that help improve how this lifecycle is deployed and how the data is organized and structured to provide clarity of information on what level of security control each tier of data analytics should be secured in alignment with. The advantage of using this method can be instrumental in aligning security of big data analytics under HIPAA law. Under the Health Insurance Portability and Accountability Act (HIPAA), patients' healthcare information must be secured throughout the workflow of health care information sharing and storage to promote an increased quality of healthcare that protects the patient's health information and well-being. The rule establishes a balance enabling important usage of information and protecting the privacy of individuals who seek healthcare and personal healing. [21]

Thus, the integration of artificial intelligence and machine learning as supporting technology tools to increase cybersecurity leadership is a dynamic approach to controlling the risks with healthcare organizations' big data analytics. Artificial intelligence algorithms can help organize the big data analytics into structured data to provide information about predictions of cyberattacks that could become threats and help define methods of risk control to decrease the impact of a successful cyberattack. Machine learning aligned with natural language processing can also help control risks of a successful cyberattack incident. The U.S. Department of Health and Human Services published a PDF presentation in July 2023, sharing valued details regarding defense and mitigation strategies against ChatGPT, phishing, malware development, and supply chain compromise. The infused tools of each of these technologies are being utilized to deploy cyberattacks. The U.S. Department of Health and Human Services report that artificial intelligence can be instrumental in providing the equal balance of support like that of a human, in correlation with perceiving, reasoning, learning, interacting within an environment, problem solving, and exercising creativity. [22] It is reported that AI can be utilized through introspection, observation, basic logic, probability reasoning, and to draw conclusions. Furthermore, it is reported that algorithms can be configured to detect patterns and provide details regarding predictions and recommendations under command, as well as can be trained to be purposeful over time. Thus, machine learning can be supportive in combating fraud, assessing social media content, and detecting facial recognition. Reliance on deep learning will enable improved information accuracy and require less human engagement.

Thus, when applying machine learning and artificial intelligence to healthcare organizations, common type of cyberattack incidents, i.e., phishing attacks, compromise of virtual privacy networks (VPNs), unauthorized access of remote desktop protocol (RDP), zero-day attacks, third-party/vendor access compromise, as well as Wi-Fi and Bluetooth compromise, there is proof that these technology tools provide leverage over cybercriminals. In fact, in January 2023, the National Institute of Standards and Technology published a new document titled Artificial Intelligence Risk Management Framework (NIST AI 100-1). [23] This framework provides detailed information regarding the significance of AI in risk management. Typically, this publication is for federal sector entities. But since healthcare organizations and institutions of higher education are held accountable to federal laws and policy regarding the protection of individuals' personal records, and because these organizations and institutions collect, assess, transmit, and store public records of personal information, this publication applies to nonfederal information systems and technology tool usage. Thus, healthcare organizations and institutions of higher education must adhere and align to this framework.

The U.S. Department of Health and Human Services reports that there is an internal and external dimension of risk management that must be clearly understood. Adhering and following the plan and design can be helpful in allowing artificial intelligence to play a powerful role in controlling and assessing the threat of a cyberattack and reducing the number of successful cyberattack incidents. [24] This cycle encompasses planning and design, collecting and processing data, building and utilizing this model, verifying and validating, deploying and usage, and operating and monitoring. When followed correctly, the recommended strategy can be useful in supporting the cybersecurity leadership needs for healthcare organizations and institutions of higher education. What has not been accomplished by former strategies of controlling risk management through human comprehension is now supported through continued support of artificial intelligence and machine learning, deep learning, and natural language processing. Thus, using big data analytics is a full-proof method of understanding the activities of human engagement in the workplace that enable vulnerabilities in knowledge sharing to become threats that support an ease of access to healthcare organizations and institution of higher education, information system weaknesses. Predictive analytics can be useful in controlling this risk factor. Knowing how personnel engage, what tools they use, and providing the training to effectively manage their role and responsibilities, are key to supporting usage of AI and machine learning to decrease future cyberattack events.

Sadly, when implementing any new strategy there are disadvantages that go unnoticed. Thus, it is essential to concern with these disadvantages to prepare a strategy to overcome the disadvantages before they become major.

When there is an absence of effective cybersecurity leadership within a healthcare organization or institution of higher education, having resources to support the needs of those in control, is a first step to being prepared. The absence of effective cybersecurity leadership and practitioners is too common. It is imperative that healthcare organizations and institutions of higher education join organizations and associations that are aligned with current trends in information sharing, regarding cyberattack incidents. Furthermore, human resource managers now carry the extra load of staying aware of these trends. Research provided by the Society of Human Resource Managers (SHRM) report that HR is a conduit between IT security and staff. HR is responsible for clarifying policy, rendering resources, and working behind the scenes to acknowledge and anticipate potential information security-related issues that will arise in all companies. [25] If Human Resource Managers do not take the initiative to ensure cybersecurity leadership is a priority for their organization, this can lead to successful cyber-attack incidents occurring. Those hired to protect and control risk within healthcare organizations and institutions of higher education, must be trained to know what their role and responsibilities are. Because IT has grown exponentially to include information systems, information security, cybersecurity, assurance, artificial intelligence, machine learning, and deep learning, there is a desperate need for these organizations and institutions to employ individuals, who are willing to continue being educated as they work through the lifecycle of the organization's or institution's cybersecurity leadership. Becoming a lifelong learner is no longer an option; it is a must to do to stay current with trends in cyberattack incidents and mitigation efforts.

5.9 Summary

Digital forensics has become a supporting tool in providing effective methods of assessing, collecting, and investigating cybercrimes deployed on computer devices, mobile devices, software, and hardware. Utilization of digital forensics tools and applications must be implemented with knowledge of how each digital forensics tool must be configured and determining, if the tool is compatible with the operating system installed on the device being investigated. Using the correct tool can be beneficial in helping collect essential information that can support the investigation as well as impact the ability to bring cybercriminals to justice. Both Snort and Wireshark are two software applications currently available that are instrumental in supporting digital forensics investigations. Keep in mind that Snort rules are used to implement Snort effectively. When Snort rules are configured incorrectly it can impact the outcome of the investigation and cripple the opportunity to collect essential information that supports an investigation. Wireshark is much simpler to utilize and easier to configure. The installation is easy and end users with little code experience can research the steps to utilize Wireshark throughout the entire usage process. Having knowledge of all operating systems – Windows, Unix/Linux, and Mac OS – is key to knowing what digital forensics tool works best with each OS. Taking time to read how operating systems differ and studying the digital forensics tools that work best with each OS can reduce the time required to correct any incorrect configurations implemented.

One of the most effective methods of digital forensics is aligning with search and seizure federal and state law and policy. Different countries have different regulations, laws, and policy regarding the usage of digital forensics tools. Therefore, it is important to have clarity on what laws, regulations, and policy, you are held accountable to. It is also important to be aware of the policies utilized within the workplace the digital forensics investigation is being conducted. This helps reduce liabilities for both the company and the investigator. Acknowledging the limits can save time and money. Building a stronger alliance with organizations and associations that provide training, conferences, and seminars regarding the current trend of digital forensics software can also be useful. While public sector has federal policy and law that must be adhered to, private sector may not be aware of these controls and implement noncompliant strategies that do not align with effective methods of usage. Beware! Utilizing these resources and understanding how each tool works will be a great way to stay ahead of cybercriminals. Otherwise, cybercriminals will continue winning the war on cybercrime.

5.10 Investigative Scenario

Ineffective deployment of digital forensics can hamper the outcome of an investigation. In healthcare organizations where desktop computers are left on and personnel are running to and from, ignoring their stations and the idea of someone walking in off the streets and gaining access to their devices can become an entrance to gain access to a computer device without authorization. When a cybersecurity leader in a healthcare organization incorrectly configures the settings on the desktop monitor to enable screen savers to immediately cover and protect access to a screen within 3 seconds, this enables strangers to gain access to desktops. Someone takes charge and gains access to a computer and enters the system, immediately plugging in a USB drive with malware installed. The malware is quickly integrated on all devices in the nurse's station without anyone being aware. What process of investigation can be implemented to begin planning to investigate the malware installed on these devices? What details must be aligned to deploy a standardized consistency of quality investigation, to prevent confusion and mistake from occurring during the collection of evidence? What evidence should be collected? How should this evidence be coded, and who should code the evidence? Having clarity of these answers plays a role in the significance of implementing an effective digital forensic investigation. But unless there is reason to assume there is an investigation needed, how will the nurses in a healthcare organization know their computers have been infected with malware? Are there laws and procedures that must be followed? Who is required to follow these laws and procedures? When there is a limit of IT personnel working in healthcare organizations, how is it determined if the current IT practitioner is knowledgeable about the installation of threats?

5.11 Discussion Questions

1. What is the title of NIST SP 800-86?
2. In what year did the United States National Institute of Standards and Technology publish NIST SP 800-86?
3. What is evidence retrieved considered?
4. Where are digital forensics collected from?
5. What is Snort often used for?
6. What Snort application should you install for Windows?
7. What is the /root command used for?
8. What does phishing emails embody?
9. What is the primary source of evidence are you seeking when examining an email header?
10. What is believed that AI can engage using?
11. Artificial intelligence algorithms can help big data analytics to become what type of data to provide information regarding predictions of cyberattacks?
12. What is Access Data FTK used for?

Glossary

Boot block – a Linux file system enveloping bootstrap code to start the system.

Carving – process of recovering fragments of file scattered across a disk.

Clusters – allocation of storage units composed of groups or sectors, i.e., 512, 1024, 2048, or 4096.

Cylinder – a column of tracks on two or more disk platters.

Data block – a Linux file block system where directories and files are located on a drive.

Digital forensics – investigative research of collected evidence from computer devices, hardware, software, mobile devices, cloud storage, USB drives for evidence purposes obtained using a search warrant and/or permission of a company to manage the custody of validating hash functions, reporting, verifying, and presenting evidence in a criminal or civil case.

Exculpatory – evidence indicating a suspect is not guilty of a crime.

Geometry – a disk drive's internal structure of platters, tracks, and sectors.

Head – the device which reads and write data to a disk drive.

Inculpatory – evidence indicating a suspect is guilty of a crime.

Inode blocks – blocks in the Linux file system containing nodes providing descriptive file or directory data, including GUI, access times, creation times, and file locations.

Packet sniffing – provides network administrators valuable information that helps them diagnose and resolve network problems.

Pharming – an email scam which utilizes DNS poisoning to redirect end users to a fake website.

Superblock – a block in the Linux file system that designates and maintain track of disk geometry and allocated space as well as manages the file system.

Tracks – concentric circles on disk platter where data is stored.

Wear-leveling – internal firmware utilized in solid state drives to ensure even wear of read/write for every memory cell.

References

[1] Nelson, B., Phillips, A., & Steuart, C. (2016). Guide to Computer Forensics and Investigations Processing Digital Evidence, (5th Ed). Cengage Learning, Boston, MA

[2] National Institute of Standards and Technology, (2006, August). Guide to Integrating Forensic Techniques into Incident Response. [PDF] Retrieved from: https://csrc.nist.gov/pubs/sp/800/86/final

[3] Nelson, B., Phillips, A., & Steuart, C. (2016). Guide to Computer Forensics and Investigations Processing Digital Evidence, (5th Ed). Cengage Learning, Boston, MA

[4] Moore, M. (2024). 23 Best Network Forensic Tools and Software [Website] Retrieved from: https://onlinedegrees.sandiego.edu/network-forensic-tools/

[5] Snort.org, (2024). What is Snort? [Website] Retrieved from: https://www.snort.org

[6] Sapphire, (2024). Snort Rule Examples and Usage: A Beginner's Guide. [Website] Retrieved from: https://www.sapphire.net/security/snort-rules-examples/

[7] Cyvatar, (2022, January 27). Writing Snort Rules with Examples and Cheat Sheet. [Website] Retrieved from: https://cyvatar.ai/write-configure-snort-rules/

[8] Wireshark, (2024). Download Wireshark. [Website] Retrieved from: https://www.wireshark.org

[9] Whitman, E. M. & Mattord, J. H. (2017). Management of Information Security (5th Ed) Cengage Learning, Boston, MA.

[10] Wireshark, (2024). 7.5 TCP Analysis, Chapter 7 Advanced Topics. [Website] Retrieved from: https://www.wireshark.org/docs/wsug_html_chunked/ChAdvTCPAnalysis.html

[11] Sherif, A. (2024, March 5). Global Market Share Held by Computer Operating Systems 2012-2014, by month. [Website] Retrieved from: https://www.statista.com/statistics/268237/global-market-share-held-by-operating-systems-since-2009/

[12] Nelson, B., Phillips, A., & Steuart, C. (2016). Guide to Computer Forensics and Investigations Processing Digital Evidence (5th Ed). Cengage Learning, Boston, MA.

[13] WinHex, (2024). Computer Forensics & Data Recovery Software, Hex Editor & Disk Editor. [Website] Retrieved from: https://www.x-ways.net/winhex/

[14] Nelson, B., Phillips, A., & Steuart, C. (2016). Guide to Computer Forensics and Investigations Processing Digital Evidence (5th Ed). Cengage Learning, Boston, MA.

[15] Tobias, E. (2021, February 15). 128- or 256-bit Encryption: Which Should I Use? [Website] Retrieved from: https://www.ubiqsecurity.com/128bit-or-256bit-encryption-which-to-use/

[16] Nelson, B., Phillips, A., & Steuart, C. (2016). Guide to Computer Forensics and Investigations Processing Digital Evidence (5th Ed). Cengage Learning, Boston, MA.

[17] Digital Intelligence, (2024). FRED Forensic Workstation. [Website] Retrieved from: https://digitalintelligence.com/products/fred/

[18] Nelson, B., Phillips, A., & Steuart, C. (2016). Guide to Computer Forensics and Investigations Processing Digital Evidence (5th Ed). Cengage Learning, Boston, MA.

[19] Oxygen Forensics, (2024). Analysis of Facebook Account Data in Oxygen Forensic Detective. [Website] Retrieved from: https://oxygen-forensics.com/en/resources/facebook-account-data-import/

[20] Batko, K. & Slezak, A. (2022, January 6). The use of Big Data Analytics in healthcare. [PDF] Retrieved from: https://www.ncbi.nlm.nih.gov/pmc/articles/PMC8733917/

[21] U.S. Department of Health and Human Services, (2024). Summary of the HIPAA Privacy Rule. [Website] Retrieved from: https://www.hhs.gov/hipaa/for-professionals/privacy/laws-regulations/index.html

[22] U.S. Department of Health and Human Services, (2023, July 13). Artificial Intelligence Cybersecurity, and the Health Sector. [PDF] Retrieved from: https://www.hhs.gov/sites/default/files/ai-cybersecurity-health-sector-tlpclear.pdf

[23] National Institute of Standards and Technology, (2023, January). Artificial Intelligence Risks Management Framework. (PDF). Retrieved from: https://nvlpubs.nist.gov/nistpubs/ai/NIST.AI.100-1.pdf

[24] U.S. Department of Health and Human Services, (2023, July 13). Artificial Intelligence Cybersecurity, and the Health Sector. [PDF] Retrieved from: https://www.hhs.gov/sites/default/files/ai-cybersecurity-health-sector-tlpclear.pdf

[25] Chavez, R. (2018, October 11). The Role of HR in Cybersecurity. [Website] Retrieved from: https://www.shrm.org/topics-tools/news/role-hr-cybersecurity

6

Artificial Intelligence for Cybersecurity Leadership

Learning Objectives

- Assess why artificial intelligence is beneficial for cybersecurity leadership.
- Investigate artificial intelligence tools for effective cybersecurity leadership.
- Distinguish machine learning and natural language processing.
- Summarize artificial intelligence ethics.

6.1 Introduction

One of the most innovative concepts of cybersecurity leadership is the integrated collaboration of artificial intelligence (AI), machine learning (ML), and natural language processing (NLP). These combined technology tools support cybersecurity leadership by helping upgrade decision-making processes that improve how baseline analytic strategies are configured to assess and deter, as well as predict future cyberattack incidents and control risk factors leading to cyberattack incident detection. Understanding each layer of artificial intelligence, machine learning, natural language processing, and the correlating abilities these technology systems provide, provides leverage for cybersecurity leaders. Research explains one useful tool and intelligent technology available for institutions of higher education cybersecurity leadership is Darktrace, which is an AI platform utilizing both AI and machine learning algorithms to identify and respond to cyber threats. [1] Research also explains AI will not replace analysts looking for threats, although it supports the ability to identify AI cyberattacks faster so cybersecurity leaders can make improved informed decisions about vulnerabilities as they occur to understand how to mitigate them. [2] Machine learning algorithms enable you to assess what activities are being deployed during a cyberattack and output future predictive analytics. This reduces the responsibilities of managers. Even though managers must know how to configure templates for policy and enforce compliance with policy. Managers must also understand machine learning and AI. Both AI and machine learning support managers in assessing the daily behavior of personnel to understand the amount of time each personnel invest in remote accessibility and understand how that remote engagement impacts system vulnerabilities. This chapter provides knowledge explaining the impact artificial intelligence has in supporting usage of predictive analytics as a reliable tool to improve the rate of cyberattack deterrence, deployed against institutions of higher education and healthcare organizations. This chapter shares knowledge explaining the role machine learning embodies in supporting cybersecurity leadership for institutions of higher education and healthcare organizations and conveys why artificial intelligence is beneficial for cybersecurity leadership. This chapter also investigates artificial intelligence tools. This enables you to distinguish machine learning and natural language processing capabilities for both healthcare organizations and institutions of higher education. A summary reiterates these findings, and an investigative study helps you assess methods of integrating AI and machine learning into your cybersecurity leadership strategies. In closing, discussion questions will help you assess your comprehension of this chapter.

Research reports that increased cyberattacks targeting colleges and universities worldwide are growing. In a global survey of 3000 IT/cybersecurity leaders, conducted by cybersecurity company Sophos, 80% of survey participants reported their institutions experienced a ransomware attack in 2023. This is a 56% increase from survey data collected in 2022. [3] Utilizing artificial intelligence to help resolve this problem is significant because AI concepts rely on an increasing method of rule-based algorithms to develop an expert system to assess various actions and deployments. [4] Research explains artificial intelligence is useful in deploying analytic applications that rely on various types of self-learning, static modeling, and/or expert systems to address direct purpose and provide a level of capability to deploy methods for distinguished multi-purpose objectives. However, when applying AI to cybersecurity leadership, it is imperative to distinguish what type of AI is essential to work effectively with institutions of higher education and healthcare organizations.

AI is divided in two applications: machine learning and deep learning. Machine learning is an algorithm trained to collect improved datasets autonomously by continually operating different types of scenarios. Deep learning correlates with machine learning, but it utilizes statistics from machine learning and applies established concepts enveloping neural network modeling to develop new complex applications of artificial intelligence. AI is defined by narrow artificial intelligence and generative artificial intelligence. Narrow artificial intelligence is not self-created and cannot derive conclusional concepts without some input from humans. It also lacks the ability to solve problems. General artificial intelligence displays creative skills, delivers context for decision-making, and can utilize past learnings to solve new unforeseen situations. Therefore, to support institutions of higher education and healthcare organizations define improved scales of cybersecurity leadership, generative artificial intelligence is best.

General artificial intelligence (GAI) can effectively incorporate variables at scale for a variety of contexts from education to medical decision-making. Generative AI correlates to artificial intelligence algorithms that develop innovative outputs defined by the data AI has been configured with. Unlike typical artificial intelligence technology developed to recognize patterns and make predictions, generative artificial intelligence designs innovative content in the form of images, text, audio, and more. [5] GAI can be supportive in helping understand patterns of behavior that correlate to understand risk factors that contribute to cyber threats. GAI is also being used by cybercriminals to deploy cyberattacks. Research reports an estimated 74% of security practitioners have experienced an increase in cyberattacks over the last year, with 84% reporting this rise is due to cyberattackers utilizing generative artificial intelligence (GAI). [6] Cybercriminals are using GAI Chatbots to deploy malware and ransomware attacks.

However, reliance on AI or GAI for cybersecurity is not without debate. In fact, a representative of the U.S government has issued a "WARNING" about usage of AI for cybersecurity. In October 2023, suggestions were made to pump the breaks on deployment of AI in cybersecurity until effective research can be deployed to ensure proof of usage will help thwart these GAI cyberattacks. Despite the U.S. Department of Homeland Security's interest in utilizing artificial intelligence to manage cyberattacks, research convey that Eric Goldstein, executive assistant director for cybersecurity at the Cybersecurity and Infrastructure Security Agency, believes agencies need to have a complete understanding of analytic data utilized to configure AI systems and to effectively test the systems for security vulnerabilities, and create sound process for disclosing vulnerabilities. [7]

Thus, one way to manage this concern is utilizing machine learning algorithms, such as logistic regression, support vector machine, and random forest/decision trees, which can be instrumental in predictive analytics to provide clarity needed to determine if usage of artificial intelligence to thwart and deter cyberattacks can be beneficial without drawbacks. [8] Machine learning logistic regression has become effective in supporting discovery of anomalies and novel patterns to improve how cybersecurity leaders understand cyber risk factors enveloped in sophisticated cyberattacks. Logistic regression is a type of machine learning approach that renders supervised learning to estimate potential assumptions about the likelihood of a target variable. [9] Using three logistic regression models – binary, multi-nominal, and ordinal, will increase the ability to understand the target variables.

Support vector machine is considered a machine learning model used to analyze data for classification and regression issues. [10] Support vector machine uniquely performs generally well, especially when applied to small sample size or learning data. The characteristics include robustness, versatility, and efficiency on datasets regardless of size, which means it can be widely used, particularly in intrusion detection. This is helpful for both institutions of higher education and healthcare organizations, IT practitioners who manage information systems, information technology, and cloud practitioners responsible for setting baselines on networks and entrance points on ports, to determine existence of irregular activity.

Random forest is an example of a regression tool used to predict intrusion detection in cybersecurity. Random forest manages high dimensional data with numerous attributes. [11] Random forest can be utilized for classification. It can also be useful for preprocessing data to help eliminate discrepancies during the initial stage of intrusion detection system installation. However, this algorithm relies on decision trees, which are constructed utilizing a bootstrap example of training data divided and chosen from a subset of traits. Utilizing this model can improve generalization efficiency and reduce overfitting. The output is developed by combining outcomes of each decision tree. Random forest is considered an excellent model for accuracy and propensity to manage omitted variables and outliers as well as resistance to overfitting.

Natural language processing encompasses artificial intelligence and linguistics with a focus to make computers comprehend statements and words used by humans in human language. [12] Two natural language processing (NLP) tasks for healthcare organizations and institutions of higher education are machine translation and automatic summarization. Natural language processing was first introduced in the 1950s as a gateway to artificial intelligence and linguistics. [13] NLP collects data from a diverse field of research, invoking developers to increase their focus on knowledge base intelligence. NLP is classified into two parts – natural language understand and natural language generation – which helps understand and generate text. NLP systems interpret the definition of words. [14] The primary goal of NLP is supporting specialties of algorithms or a system. Metrics of NLP assess an algorithm system and enable the integration of language comprehension and language creation. A primary objective of NLP is interpreting, analyzing, and manipulating natural language data in correlation with different algorithms, tools, and methods. This provides an improved understanding of words, text, images, and files commonly used by previous cybercriminal attackers, in previous cyberattacks, targeting institutions of higher education and healthcare organizations. This information can classify search patterns for algorithms to compile supporting analytics to define specifics about the potential method of attack deployed by those cybercriminals.

However, there are challenges embodied in natural language data that must be considered. This can impact the ability to achieve the primary objective, which is to understand patterns of cybercriminal attack methods. Thus, two contributing factors of NLP that must be understood are machine translation and automatic summarization. Machine translation is the automatic translation of one human language to another. Machine translation has two methods: rule-based and corpus-based. Rule-based machine translation methods use bilingual dictionaries and manually written rules to translate source language texts into target language texts. [15] Corpus-based machine translation methods embody three known methods: example-based machine translation, statistical machine translation, and neural machine translation.

A primary concept of machine translation is to develop an automated system to translate a natural source language into a target language via bilingual dictionaries, algorithm-based configurations, and corpus and neural systems. [16] Machine translation technology thrives to support humans' ability to translate accurately large scales of text or speech into various languages with little effort. But this process cannot be fully achieved without the input of human interaction. To ensure accuracy of language translation, someone must intervene to pre-edit all text input and deploy post-editing. This ensures the readability of the final translation product. Machine translation first gained popularity in the 1950s and was considered a word-to-word translation, resulting in the need to deteriorate communication barriers between military and intelligence communities.

Initially, the idea of using a three-stage process for translating between languages with computers, should include analyzing, transferring, and synthesizing. Unfortunately, research conveys this did not progress as anticipated. Years later, machine translation processing was modified using a rule-based concept, in which the role of the machine is to provide grammatical rules defined by bilingual dictionaries and grammar-detecting error software. [17] Then, statistical machine translation was developed using sets of algorithms to configure computers to predict accurate texts defined by human translation. The final stage integrates advantages from previous approaches and provide accuracy to translate outputs created by machine translation.

Today, the most relied on machine translation tools are Google translate, Hybrid machine translate, Amazon translate, Alexa translate, and Microsoft translator. Each one of these translation tools provide unique services, but they each translate words and language into various other languages. The advantage of utilizing machine translation includes providing quick translation responses without needing to vex a machine to translate. This creates cost efficiency for large volumes of data translation and improves adaptability The disadvantage of machine translation includes quality limitations, culture linguistics challenges, limited textual comprehension, and privacy concerns. [18]

Automatic summarization is the development of a shortened version of a textual document by a computer program containing the most important content of the original document. [19] Automatic summarization provides rapid concise clarity on key facts or concepts about something or someone. Automatic summarization also provides clarity of key variables within a structured version of a textual document. This helps readers comprehend the text. Manual conversion or summarization is an arduous task; therefore, automation is required. Automation can be accomplished through artificial intelligence technology. [20] Manual text summarization requires a lot of time to assess and can be quite expensive and laborious to achieve. Thus, automation has gained popularity. Two types of automation summarization are extraction and abstraction.

Extraction summarization compiles sentences from documents defined by a scoring function to establish a coherent summary. [21] This includes identifying valuable parts of text and compiling portions of content to create a condensed version of that content. Extraction summarization envelops important sentences from input that embodies a single document of multiple documents. Abstractive summarization produces a summary via interpreting text utilizing an advanced natural language technique that creates shorter text. Using part of an original document involves rephrasing sentences and incorporating information from such text to develop summaries. Abstract summarization envelopes core information in the input and is linguistically fluent. Abstract summarization is a challenging task, much more difficult than extraction summarization. Research reports that abstraction summarization can be impacted by repetition and semantic irrelevance, which creates grammatical errors and inaccurate reflection of the main text source. Thus, these disadvantages can impact the accuracy of analytics collected from algorithms if not understood by institutions of higher education and healthcare organization cybersecurity leaders. This can impact their ability to effectively assess predictive analytics to determine the success rate of cyberattacks, when determining where those attacks originate. This can also impede on their ability to implement effective cybersecurity mitigation strategies.

Luckily, there are several types of AI summarization tools available, including Jasper, Smodin, QuillBot, Scholarcy, and Notta. The advantage of automatic summarization is that it is scalable. It is comprehensible. It also enables a clear summarization of text in different formats.

So, when hypothesizing challenges for automatic processing of NLP, it is determined that without input from human interaction of data into machines, the ability to effectively translate data from one language into another clearly, is impossible without inaccuracy. This can impact the ability for machine translation to be useful. The same can be applied to automatic summarization. There are common translation difficulties defined by culture linguistic. This impedes the ability to derive at a precise understanding of language translation too often. Thus, leading to misinterpretation of collected data.

When applied to cybersecurity leadership in institutions of higher education, many institutions worldwide who deliver asynchronous learning platforms, and who are facing cyberattack risks, may not have the information needed to implement improved cybersecurity leadership. Using natural language processing machine translation can be a vital asset to supporting the needs of these institutions. And although the United States, United Kingdom, and parts of Asia are working in concert with institutions of higher education, to provide clarity of methods to deter cyberattacks via recommended guidelines and policy, as well as mitigation strategies, the lack of trained and support rendered by information systems and information technology practitioners, cripples the ability for these institutions and organizations to effectively adopt strategies currently used abroad. The challenge rests in machine translation, i.e., words having multiple meanings, sentences with multiple grammatical structures, uncertainty about what a pronoun refers to, and additional problems of grammar that impact the perceived interpretation of how strategies are assessed and aligned with the needs of one institution of higher education in one country to thwart cybercrimes, and the needs of other institutions of higher education in other countries to do the same.

Thus, the proposed application to help decrease these challenges can be integrated to deploy automatic processing of the NLP challenges identified in both machine translation and automatic summarization. To help overcome this challenge, Amazon offers Amazon Translate. This application delivers

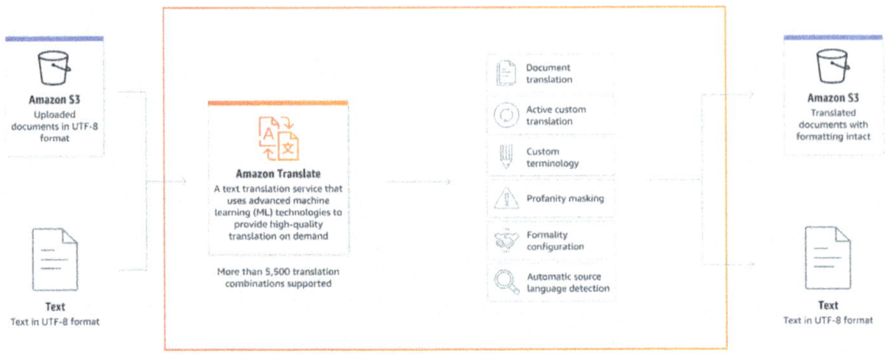

Figure 6.1 Amazon Web Services (2024). Amazon Translate. [Website] Retrieved from: https://aws.amazon.com/translate/

accurate and continuous translation for various use cases. This application enables developers to build batch translation capabilities using a single API as well as customize machine learning output that defines a brand name, model name, and usage of unique terms. The embedded image (Figure 6.1) below shows details of the translation process delivered by Amazon:

Data input transitions through the translation service utilizing advanced machine learning technology that renders quality translation on demand. This helps with custom terminology, profanity masking, and automatic source language detection. The output is always formatted accurately. This service is beneficial in supporting the needs of institutions of higher education in combating the threat of cyberattacks. The broad language translation service works with 75 languages: Afrikaans, Albanian, Amharic, Arabic, Armenian, Azerbaijani, Bengali, Bosnian, Bulgarian, Chinese (Simplified), Catalan, Chinese (Traditional), Croatian, Czech, Danish, Dari, Dutch, English, Estonian, Finnish, French, French (Canada), Georgian, German, Greek, Gujarati, Haitian Creole, Hausa, Hebrew, Hindi, Hungarian, Icelandic, Indonesian, Irish, Italian, Japanese, Kannada, Kazakh, Korean, Latvian, Lithuanian, Macedonian, Malay, Malayalam, Maltese, Mongolian, Marathi, Norwegian, Farsi (Persian), Pashto, Polish, Portuguese, Portuguese (Portugal), Punjabi, Romanian, Russian, Serbian, Sinhala, Slovak, Slovenian, Somali, Spanish, Spanish (Mexico), Swahili, Swedish, Filipino Tagalog, Tamil, Telugu, Thai, Turkish, Ukrainian, Urdu, Uzbek, Vietnamese, and Welsh. And also supports 5000 translation combinations. Using this as an automatic summarization and machine translate service can help decrease challenges commonly known with usage of machine translation service providers.

Using natural language processing in alignment with machine translation and automatic summarization, despite the challenges these two systems embody, can benefit institutions incapable of having access to NLP translation services worldwide. Having clarity on the challenges of machine translation and partnering with a service and product provider, who renders quality services in translation, can be a resolution to the growing problem when there is an absence of access to reliable, trusted, and quality information systems and information technology practitioner guidelines. Because the United States Cybersecurity Infrastructure Security Agency and the National Institute of Standards and Technology continually develop new training and recommended guidelines to deter cyberattacks. Integrating Amazon Translate in institutions of higher education abroad as a medium to help these institutions acquire the needed support to protect their information systems and technology from unauthorized intrusion, bridges the gap to accessing the much-needed translated recommended guidelines and strategies published by the National Institute of Standards and Technology. Being able to translate English recommended guidelines into 5000 translated combinations across 75 languages worldwide, certainly is the best alternative to supporting the needs of these institutions in connecting with United States federally regulated recommended guidelines, to secure information systems, using encryption and risks management framework in correlation with artificial intelligence, machine learning, and natural language processing.

In addition, understanding how to investigate artificial intelligence tools for effective cybersecurity leadership is important. Research reports that Darktrace is helpful in detecting anomalous threats and renders support across cloud, email, Internet of Things (IoT), remote endpoints, and networks. [22] Darktrace provides incident investigation reporting. This application is useful for potential issues that can ease pass network administration predetermined baselines. This helps catch potential threats as they occur, to minimize the success of an actual exploit. Additionally, Darktrace's artificial intelligence algorithms continue to understand and assess evolving threat landscapes, which helps identify known and unknown threats, as well as detect irregular activities that may have been ignored previously.

Another artificial intelligence tool that is recommended for cybersecurity leadership is Check Point Software, which provides network monitoring and security. This application is recommended because it is integrated with artificial intelligence that predicts and prevents attacks on networks, cloud systems, and endpoints. Research explains that reliance on machine learning engines enable this application to identify and block zero-day threats. This helps lower the cost of security, while increasing assessment services, including cyber risks, penetration testing, supply chain risk assessment, IoT risk assessment, and ransomware readily assessment. [23] While these services and products resemble Darktrace, it is important to acknowledge that what works with one institution of higher education or healthcare organization, may not necessarily align with the technology utilized by another. Things to consider when determining compatibility of third-party services and products are the scale of usage and the possibility that such services or products may not be equipped to work with current network servers, operating systems, cloud applications, or software utilized for daily business communication and operation. Research reports that compatibility issues happen when devices differ, or software systems differ and are unable to effectively communicate and operate together as expected. When there are differences in protocols, configurations, updates needed, and standards of usage, lacking knowledge of each of these as it relates to any system utilized, will impact the ability for the system to operate correctly. Furthermore, compatibility concerns can create havoc for healthcare organizations and institutions of higher education by increasing downtime, invoking reduction of productivity, and reducing an overall return on investment. Compatibility issues can also create reputational damage. [24]

Another artificial intelligence tool that can support cybersecurity leadership for institutions of higher education or healthcare organizations is developed by Trellix, which is like Darktrace and Check Point Software, because Trellix delivers ransomware protection, data security, network security, email security, and endpoint security. Trellix is recommended because this service and product provider, delivers partnerships for managers to help balance the risk control and provides the quality of support needed to guide institutions of higher education and healthcare organizations into a safe and secure phase of cybersecurity leadership. When applied with cross services, adding additional layers of security and management partnering is a dynamic defense for an organization that has a high number of employees operating across a large-scale parameter, with a small IT staff. Having the support of a professional and respected third-party service provider can tremendously improve the ability to successfully defeat cybercriminals.

In partnership with machine learning tools that can be supportive for cybersecurity leadership, you also must consider IBM QRadar Analysis, which provides dynamic predictability results derived from incident and risks analysis. This is important because it reduces the timeline to investigate a cyberattack incident. Research reports that institutions of higher education often are slow in remediating and mitigating cyberattack incidents once they are discovered. Research explains that the average recovery timeline is

49 days for institutions of higher education. This creates financial hardship and causes operational disruption and possible reputational damage. [25] IBM QRadar Analysis deploys automation and increases commonalities in investigations rendering actionable recommendations for analysts and integrates a SIEM (security information event management) system that delivers increased IT security support. IBM provides several QRadar tools, including incident forensics, data storage, and synchronization. Data storage and synchronization is beneficial for resiliency and data recovery. This is also useful in supporting and assessing human error incidents. As stated previously, human error incidents are 88% cause of most cyber incidents in the workplace.

Furthermore, machine learning tools are useful because they align with deep learning. As pointed out previously, this is a benefit in supporting cybersecurity. This application partners with institutions of higher education and healthcare organizations by modifying endpoint security from a reactive to a predictive approach that protects against known and unknown threats. [26] This application delivers effective endpoint protection and enforces data execution prevention, stack pivot, and heap spray allocation. Understanding machine learning applications and tools and how they work in comparison with artificial intelligence software and information systems and networks, is crucial to understanding the scale of defense these applications can deploy and the abilities embodied in utilizing these tools. No matter how many tools of defense implemented, there is no 100% way to stop a cyberattack from happening. [27]

For instance, Sophos is another way of deploying cloud as an application to increase security and ransomware threat defense. Sophos professes that it prevents the exploitation of vulnerabilities and decreases malicious behavior. This service provider configures a system that adapts a defense that is modified with all changing attack behavior. It is easy to configure and deploy. But like each of the other applications discussed and investigated, having clarity on the requirements to ensure accuracy and usage of these tools is necessary.

Thus, as pointed out previously, understanding natural language processing (NLP) for cybersecurity leadership is important because cyberattacks are deployed globally, and language differences from one country to another can impact the ability to assess the potential risk factors obviously displayed in an attack deployed in the English-speaking language but not necessarily understood in Chinese, Mandarin, Arabic, Russian, Spanish, or French. When examining the most prevalent languages used in cyberattacks deployed from countries like China and Russia, having natural language processing tools are useful in cyber defense.

Utilizing data analytics is essential to predictive analytics, which is instrumental in helping institutions of higher education and healthcare organizations reduce the potential risk of being victimized by a cyberattack, because patterns deployed in previous attacks toward competitors can be assessed and can be adaptable to deterrence methods implemented by these systems. This is what makes data analytics important. Data analytics enables organizations to clean, analyze, interpret, and visualize details compiled from data collected to help discover problems that can lead to cyberattack incidents. Much like baseline configurations for network servers and systems, using data analytics to predetermine the possibility of understanding patterns of text messages, email messages, and documents saved and transmitted across an organization's network, may not necessarily be the approach to controlling all risks associated with technology usage. But this approach has grown substantially in use because it has provided clarity on the role natural language processing delivers in understanding the correlation between cyberattackers and attack victims.

Although integrating artificial intelligence, machine learning, and natural language processing is innovative and an effective strategy to control risk factors enveloped in usage of technology tools, including software, hardware, Internet-Of-Things (IoT), Wi-Fi, telecommunications, printers, mobile devices, and ChatGPT. The concern of ethics arises, invoking a need to assess what rights healthcare organizations and institutions of higher education have utilizing these mediums to increase their cybersecurity leadership. One of the leading healthcare ethical policies is the United States Health Insurance Probability and Accountability Act (HIPAA). This federal law was mandated in 1996 with the purpose of establishing national standards to protect private patient healthcare information from being disclosed without a patient's consent and knowledge. [28] Under this United States federal law, the privacy rule, plays a key role in how personal healthcare information is collected, shared, and stored, both in transmission electronically and at rest. Thus, when utilizing technology tools and artificial intelligence, machine learning, and natural language processing applications, the rules become double edged because patients must provide their consent prior to their healthcare information being shared with anyone. This creates a burden of proof for healthcare organizations, who are implementing innovative concepts of protection and cybersecurity leadership to govern and control risk factors relating to the security and privacy of their patient's healthcare information.

According to the United States Center for Disease Control and Prevention, both healthcare providers and health plans are accountable to the privacy rule. Healthcare providers include all healthcare providers, regardless of their size in personnel and operation, and the usage of electronically transmitted healthcare information relating to transactions, including claims, benefit eligibility requirements, and referral authorization. Health plans include information relating to health, dental, vision, and prescription drug insurers, HMO, employer- sponsored group health plans, government- and church-sponsored healthcare plans, and long-term healthcare insurers. However, research explains that employers who administer a health plan for less than 50 employees is not a covered entity and is not accountable under the HIPAA law. This means, business associates rendering data analytics for cybersecurity leadership are not held to the laws and restrictions of HIPAA.

Thus, as mentioned previously when sharing details about NIST A.I. 100-1 Artificial Intelligence Risk Management Framework, organizations are responsible for the integration and usage of AI, machine learning, and deep learning to improve their cyberattack mitigation strategies. While HIPAA is a primary governing framework invoking healthcare organizations to enhance security measures to protect patient's sensitive information. It is important that healthcare organizations, IT personnel are adhering to all proactive policies mandated by federal and international law, and ensuring they are maintaining effective written records regarding the auditing of the usage of AI, machine learning, and natural language processing tools to support their usage of these applications for cyber defense. Otherwise, this can raise issues of ethics and integrity.

Since 2020 debates have grown regarding the integration of AI and machine learning applications for medical diagnoses and healthcare imagery. This debate enhances the patient consent rule and places healthcare organizations in a bind holding them accountable, even though AI may render inaccurate medical results. This creates the clause of usage of AI in medical treatment and diagnosis, which must be emphasized in healthcare organization policies. Ensuring patients are aware of the consent to share their personal medical records across AI-powered services, such as third-party Chatbot providers systems, protects healthcare organizations from product liability and being held accountable under HIPAA and the Electronic Privacy Protection Act.

Thus, ineffective configuration of AI tools and machine learning applications when used for cybersecurity leadership can create some stir, but unless large databases of information are stolen through a Chatbot system, the healthcare organization that was victimized is not necessarily going to face steep penalties. This places the responsibility into the hands of the consumer, so to speak, because consumers are warned by the healthcare providers about the usage of AI for medical and security purposes, and the consent of consumers to receive services through such healthcare organizations remains protected. While this may be beneficial in the utilization of AI and machine learning for cybersecurity leadership in the United States or Europe, other countries are still negotiating terms for how AI can be integrated and how laws will be applied to protect citizen's right to privacy when it pertains to AI and machine learning as culprits in a cybersecurity breach, where cybercriminals gain access to patient's personal healthcare information during the cyberattack.

One incident where this is prevalent occurred in Australia, in February 2022, when the Australian Clinical Labs, a registered Security Exchange corporation who renders medical pathology services, was victimized by cybercriminals through a third-party access. Although a forensics investigation was deployed, it was concluded there was no vital impact resulting from this incident. However, reports were published publicly, and the corporation was eventually notified by the Office of Australian Information Commissioners that a formal civil liabilities investigation was filed in the Federal Courts of Australia. Since the data breach occurred in February 2022, Australian Clinical Labs can only be fined A$2.2 million because the Office of Australian Information Commissioners are prioritizing the swiftness of response to cybersecurity incidents as they occur. And because the Australian Clinical Labs neglected to acknowledge that a cyberattack occurred, they are being held accountable. But in December 2022, the Australian legislature enhanced the maximum penalty for "serious" contraventions of the Privacy Act to A$50 million. [29]

Another incident occurred in the Netherlands in January 2024, relating to 1.3 million exposed medical records in an unsecured database hosted by Google, a third-party cloud computing service provider. It was determined by Google that accountability for this breach fell into the hands of the healthcare organization, which neglected to implement effective usage and configuration control framework to avoid being victimized by cybercriminals. Research explains that this database lacked password protection for documents coded with the name and logo of Coronalab.eu, that is owned by Microbe & Lab, a medical laboratory based in Amsterdam. [30] Assuming cloud computing as the choice of security was a good idea, but the healthcare organization should have taken steps to ensure usage of the cloud computing application was secured and impenetrable. Neglecting to enforce effective implementation and configuration of system services is one of the leading causes for system failures. Thus, healthcare organizations utilizing third-party services for database storage and information sharing, must increase their knowledge of the services and applications relied on and implement better training for those hired to manage their usage of third-party applications.

As mentioned throughout this chapter, utilizing external services and products for cybersecurity leadership in healthcare or institutions of higher education, requires strict compliance regulatory and consistent upgrading of services as required by the service or product provider. Neglecting to do so will impact the outcome of cyber incidents as they occur and after they are resolved. When the public is made aware of these incidents, it can create fear and distrust in the ability of the healthcare organization or institution of higher education to effectively secure the information provided by consumers. Value is invested in information more today than ever before. When organizations neglect to see the significance in managing the risk factors enveloped in utilizing third-party applications, it can be costly. It can also impact an organization when it lacks the ability to work in concert as a group to make informed decisions that impact the overall success of the organization.

One way to help organizations improve their decision-making processing in determining how to implement AI, machine learning, and natural language processing, is utilizing collective intelligence. This is a good way to improve decision-making when determining how to implement improved cybersecurity leadership. Research explains that collective intelligence focuses on group decision-making to enable innovation to develop. This development enables groups to make improved decisions that provide leverage over competitors and can help reduce excessive budget spending. Collective intelligence is divided into three forms: cognition, cooperation, and coordination. When applied effectively, group synergy enables improved problem solving and decision-making, which can help determine what scale of AI or machine learning, and natural language processing will best serve the needs of the organization to improve their cybersecurity leadership. When people contribute their experience and knowledge in decision-making, it improves the overall outcome of the objectives they seek individually and as a group. However, it is important to consider the disadvantages that can arise from reliance on collective intelligence when it is not effective. Research explains that usage of computerized decision-making systems can often sometimes result in information overload. Since computerized decision-making systems analyze all areas of a problem, end users with little training in understanding decision-making processes, may remain entangled in what should be considered beneficial and what should not. After all, not every bite of information is necessary in decision-making. But when it's present, a decision-maker finds it difficult to ignore information that is not a priority. [31] Furthermore, people tend to become dependent on decision-making support systems and neglect to think on their own. This can be crippling and hinder innovation and usage of individual ideas. Another drawback is devaluation of subjectivity, which means that a decision support system's rational decision-making ability impacts the basis of objectivity. After all, there can be an issue with overemphasis of decision-making tool usage. Thus, it is invaluable to ensure team players working with decision-making systems are aware of the limitations of these systems and are not ignoring problems that could result in usage of these systems as the sole source of idea conceptualization. Therefore, when determining if artificial intelligence, machine learning, and natural language processing can be useful is supporting cybersecurity leadership for healthcare organizations and institutions of higher education, it is instrumental in understanding what scale of AI should be utilized and how it can benefit an organization, with little complications and liabilities. The same applies to usage of machine learning and natural language processing. Applying any form of artificial intelligence to make collective intelligent decisions for cybersecurity cannot be achieved without making firm human decisions defined by research and rationale of this research. Doing so will increase the ability to make a firm decision about the abilities AI will render, and the organization can implement policy that protects it from liabilities, when something goes wrong. Most importantly, is knowing how to align usage of AI applications with the jurisdiction of AI usage. What works in the United States does not work in all countries and vice versa.

6.2 Summary

Artificial intelligence (AI), machine learning (ML), and natural language processing (NLP) are collective technology systems and applications that can be useful in supporting the need for improved predictive analytics in the decision-making process for institutions of higher education and healthcare organizations. When applied effectively, artificial intelligence operates to support the inability of many cybersecurity leaders to make informed decisions regarding possibilities of the potential risk of being victimized by a cyberattack. Artificial intelligence is programmed to support human thinking. Thus, it is not without fault and can play a role in supporting a cyberattack occurrence. If improperly configured, AI can be a catastrophic tool that impacts the outcome of an organization's ability to thwart and deter cyberattacks successfully. Machine learning when applied correctly can also be a benefit to support institutions of higher education and healthcare organizations in thwarting and deterring cyberattacks. But like AI, machine learning must be understood and configured to provide the objectives sought, or the results may not meet the demands. Utilizing natural language processing in concert with AI and machine learning can establish a system that can make informed decisions regarding language command prompts to improve defense and predictive analytics, when cybercriminals are developing attack methods to deploy attack applications, i.e., malware and ransomware. After all, with the integration of Chatbot AI applications, cybercriminals are programming these applications to attack organizations with hope of avoiding capture with minimum risks. Unfortunately, not all IT practitioners working in healthcare organizations or institutions of higher education are knowledgeable on how to effectively assess the potential risk of utilizing third-party services and products, which is a result of many cyberattacks deployed today.

Unless increased knowledge sharing continues, the growth of AI and machine learning to deploy cyberattacks against institutions of higher education and healthcare organization will soar, and the number of victims impacted will paint an idea that ineffective cybersecurity is being deployed in healthcare organizations and institutions of higher education worldwide. This will prove to cybercriminals that these territories are reliable for victimization and will continue pursuing these organizations and institutions without fear of penalty. Thus, it is imperative that improved efforts are implemented in how AI, machine learning, and natural language processing are assessed, configured, and utilized as cybersecurity tools to decrease the growing threat of cyberattacks. Implementing policy and compliance regulation aligning with federal law and policy both domestically and internationally is key. Staying connected with organizations and industry leaders who have the resources and who are doing the research for you, will provide the current knowledge needed to ensure healthcare organizations and institutions of higher education, stay aware of the potential risks and benefits of utilizing these applications and tools to support cybersecurity leadership.

When partnering with third-party service and product providers for artificial intelligence, machine learning, and natural language processing applications and tools, it is imperative to understand what service and product provider is reliable, and the risk enveloped is partnering with a service or product provider. Doing so can decrease the probability of being victimized by a weakness in a service or product that is not effectively configured and can hinder the ability for an organization to effectively implement a successful cyber defense, utilizing these tools. Keeping in alignment with the recommended guidelines of NIST A.I. 100-1 Artificial Intelligence Risk Management Framework and additional NIST special publications can support the inability of many IT practitioners lacking the current trend in utilization of AI and machine learning for cybersecurity leadership. Otherwise, you risk being victimized.

6.3 Investigative Scenario

University of Bellevue Hospital operates in Bellevue, Michigan, with 8000 employees, across a campus of 87,000 square feet. This major research center delivers primary and specialty care, and hosts 600 licensed beds. Services are provided for women, children, psychiatric and mental healthcare, and an emergency department. Utilization of Wi-Fi is delivered through satellite Internet services provided by Star Quill, and usage of VoIP telecommunication systems support their land-line communication. There are 10 IT staff employees who work two shifts, 6:00 am to 2:00 pm and 2:00 pm to 10:00 pm. During the hours of 10:00 pm to 5:30 am, the network system is operating autonomously, and the IT director and two IT managers are on remote accessibility, utilizing a 24-hour on call alert alarm system, which chimes their phones in case of emergency. The hospital has not experienced a cyberattack, so the concept of being victimized is not a reality, although the director of IT has implemented IT training as a model for awareness among all IT staff members. This training has encompassed awareness of cyberattack modes, i.e., Distributed Denial of Service Attacks (DDoSA), phishing attacks, ransomware attacks, viruses, worms, Trojans, and MySQL injections. Training has been rendered to personnel working on desktop computers and laptops, around the clock, who are aware of phishing attack methods, email attack methods, and DDoSA. Personnel are also aware of ransomware attacks and malware attacks. However, usage of cloud services for cybersecurity leadership has not been implemented, and the hospital IT director doesn't feel that the current staff is capable of managing the transition of on-premises database to the cloud and has been hesitant to impose the risks of doing so because he is unsure if presenting the risks will outweigh the benefits, when presented to the executive leadership of the hospital, who must play a role in supporting this decision. Thus, the IT director conducts research and provides a detailed outline of the risks associated with transitioning from an on-premises network to a full cloud-based application. He believes this will provide some leverage over the potential risks of maintaining an on-premises network that requires consistent hands-on cybersecurity application tool installation and updating, that his current staff is not fully prepared to manage as the hospital grows and more marketing increases, putting the hospital in the news and making them more of a target for cybercriminals to attack.

Therefore, Darktrace is being considered for usage because it is helpful in detecting anomalous threats and provides support across usage of cloud, email, Internet of Things (IoT), remote endpoints, and networks. Darktrace's artificial intelligence algorithms continue to understand and assess evolving threat landscapes and help identify known and unknown threats by detecting irregular activities. Trellix will be applied because it enables the hospital to implement an effective ransomware deterrence application and increase the layer of security the hospital requires. What else is missing to provide the hospital enough protection against cyberattack victimization? How can it be determined that usage of these applications and cloud will provide the layer of security this hospital seeks? What NIST policies must be considered and why? What federal laws, domestic and international, must be assessed and align with the hospital's reliance on cloud as a primary application for data storage and transmission?

6.4 Discussion Questions

1. What relies on an increasing method of rule-based algorithms to develop an experts system to assess various actions and deployments?
2. What is algorithm trained to collect improved datasets autonomously by operating different types of scenarios?
3. What can effectively incorporate variables at scale for a variety of contexts from education to medical decision-making?
4. Who issued a warning about usage of AI for cybersecurity?
5. What can random forest be utilized for?
6. Why does machine translation technology thrive to support humans?
7. What are the two parts of natural language processing?
8. What are the names of two AI summarization tools mentioned in this chapter?
9. What is NIST A.I. 100-1?
10. What is HIPAA?
11. What year did machine translation first gain popularity?
12. What machine learning tool provides dynamic predictability results that derive from incident and risks analysis?

Glossary

Algorithms – mathematical formula utilized to modify unencrypted data into detailed information.

Artificial intelligence – computerized systems that require human intelligence input through command prompts and delivered through robotic machines to deploy responses as opposed to natural intelligence.

Generative artificial intelligence – innovative artificial intelligence that can produce new innovations such as conversation, share stories, display images, videos, and share music.

Machine learning – computer system capable of understanding and adapting to instructions without being given explicit instructions, by relying on algorithms and statistical methods to analyze and acquire inferences from patterns of data.

Machine translation – a method of processing artificial intelligence to automate translation of text from one language to another absent human interaction.

NARROW artificial intelligence – deploys specific tasks or a set of closely related tasks, and thrives to replicate human intelligence humans can, but limited in scope.

Natural language processing – machine learning technology that enables computers to interpret, modify, and understand human languages.

References

[1] Abdullahi, A. (2023, December 19). 20 Best AI Security Software for 2024. [Website] https://www.eweek.com/artificial-intelligence/best-ai-security-tools/

[2] Miller, A. J. (2020, March 3). 3 Ways Artificial Intelligence Can Improve Campus Security. [Website] https://edtechmagazine.com/higher/article/2020/03/3-ways-artificial-intelligence-can-improve-campus-cybersecurity-perfcon

[3] Collins, T. (2024, January 1). Network Resilience in Schools: How Out of Band Management Can Safeguard Educational Processes. [Website] https://www.campussafetymagazine.com/blogs/network-resilience-in-schools-how-out-of-band-management-can-safeguard-educational-processes/

[4] Casey, T. (2018, December). The Real Facts About Artificial Intelligence [White paper]. Teradata Consulting, Automating Intelligence Series. https://assets.teradata.com/resourceCenter/downloads/WhitePapers/EB10271_POD.pdf?_gl=1*ejruzj*_ga*MTc3ODMwNDkxOC4x-

NjI2ODAzNzM5*_ga_7PE2TMW3FE*MTYyNjg4NDMyOC4yL-jAuMTYyNjg4NDMyOC4w

[5] Routley, N. (2023, February 6). What is generative AI? [Website] Retrieved from: https://www.weforum.org/agenda/2023/02/generative-ai-explain-algorithms-work/

[6] Security Staff, (2023, August 29). Study finds increase in cybersecurity attacks fueled by generative AI. [Website] Retrieved from: https://www.securitymagazine.com/articles/99832-study-finds-increase-in-cybersecurity-attacks-fueled-by-generative-ai

[7] Nash, K. (2023, October 18). Federal Cyber Chief Tells Agencies to Tap Breaks on AI. [Website] Retrieved from: https://www.wsj.com/articles/federal-cyber-chief-tells-agencies-to-tap-brakes-on-ai-343cbe28

[8] Yeboah-Ofori, A., Shareeful, I., Lee, W.S., Shamszaman, U.Z, Muhammad, K., Altaf, M., Al-Rakhami, M. (2021, July 9). Cyber Threat Predictive Analytics for Improving Cyber Supply Chain Security. [PDF] https://ieeexplore.ieee.org/stamp/stamp.jsp?tp=&arnumber=9448097

[9] Gonaygunta, H. (2023, January). Machine Learning Algorithms for Detection of Cyber Threats Using Logistic Regression. [PDF] http://tinyurl.com/y6hpudrk

[10] Ngueajio, K.M., Washington, G., Rawat, B.D. & Ngueabou, Y. (2022, September 12). Intrusion Detection Systems Using Support Vector Machines on the KDDCUP'99 and NSL-KDD Datasets: A Comprehensive Study. [PDF] https://arxiv.org/abs/2209.05579

[11] Hadi Ali, A.A. & Hadi, M. A. (2024, February 16). Improving cybersecurity with random forest algorithm-based big data intrusion detection system: A performance analysis. [PDF] Retrieved from: https://pubs.aip.org.aip/acp/article-abstract/3051/1/040012/3266034/Improving-cybersecurity-with-random-forest?redirectedFrom=fulltext

[12] Khurana, D., Koli, A., & Singh, S. (2023, July 14). Natural language processing: state of the art, current trends and challenges. [Website] https://www.ncbi.nlm.nih.gov/pmc/articles/PMC9281254/

[13] Nadkarni, M.P., Machado-Ohno, L. & Chapman, W.W. (2011, July 6). Natural language processing: an introduction. [PDF] https://academic.oup.com/jamia/article/18/5/544/829676?login=false

[14] Khurana, D., Koli, A., & Singh, S. (2023, July 14). Natural language processing: state of the art, current trends and challenges. [Website] https://www.ncbi.nlm.nih.gov/pmc/articles/PMC9281254/

[15] Wang, H., Wu, H., He, Z., Huang, L., Church, W.K. (2021, July 14). Progress in Machine Translation. [PDF] https://www.sciencedirect.com/science/article/pii/S2095809921002745

[16] Mohsen, A.M., Althebi, S. & Albahooth, M. (2023, August 1). A scientometric study of three decades of machine translation research: Trending issues, hotspot research, and co-citation analysis. [PDF] https://www.tandfonline.com/doi/epdf/10.1080/23311983.2023.2242620?needAccess=true

[17] Sharda, R., Delen, D. & Turban, E, (2020). Analytics, data science, & artificial intelligence: Systems for decision support (11th ed). Pearson. New York, N.Y., p. 402

[18] Speak Your Language Administration (2023, August 14). The Advantages and Disadvantages of Machine Translation. [Website] https://translationsandinterpretations.com.au/blog/the-advantages-and-disadvantages-of-machine-translation/

[19] Sharda, R., Delen, D. & Turban, E, (2020). Analytics, data science, & artificial intelligence: Systems

[20] Fitria, N.T. (2023, July). Using Manual and Automatic Summarization: What Should Students Consider in Writing a Summary? [PDF] https://unkartur.ac.id/journal/index.php/electrum/article/download/140/160

[21] Gonclaves, L. (2020, April 11). Automatic Text Summarization with Machine Learning -An Overview. [Website] https://medium.com/luisfredgs/automatic-text-summarization-with-machine-learning-an-overview-68ded5717a25

[22] Abdullahi, A. (2023, December 19). 20 Best AI Security Software for 2024. [Website] Retrieved from: https://www.eweek.com/artificial-intelligence/best-ai-security-tools/

[23] Check Point (2024). Assess Security Evaluation and Pentesting. [Website] Retrieved from: https://igs.checkpoint.com/categories/assess

[24] Wang, F. (2023, April 18). Compatibility Issues with Different Operating Systems or Network Hardware. [Website] Retrieved from: https://www.linkedin.com/pulse/compatibility-issues-different-operating

[25] Itro, D. (2023, October 30). 8 Considerations When Establishing Cybersecurity in Higher Education. [Website] Retrieved from: https://er.educause.edu/articles/sponsored/2023/10/8-considerations-when-establishing-cybersecurity-in-higher-education

[26] Choudhury, A. (2021, March 3). Top 8 Machine Learning Tools for Cybersecurity. [Website] Retrieved from: https://analyticsindiamag.com/top-8-machine-learning-tools-for-cybersecurity/

[27] Sonar, M. (2023, March 2). Why Can't Organizations Be 100% Secure? [Website] Retrieved from: https://mediasonar.com/2023/03/02/100-percent-secure/

[28] Centers for Disease Control and Prevention, (n.d.). Health Insurance Portability and Accountability Act of 1996 [Website] retrieved from: https://www.cdc.gov/phlp/publications/topic/hipaa.html

[29] Kurth, A.H. (2023, November 15). Australian Privacy Regulator Sues in Data Breach Case [Website] Retrieved from: https://www.lexology.com/library/detail.aspx?g=8c79b991-ea08-4adf-ba2f-18cbec28fc5d

[30] McGee, K.M. (2024, January 23). Medical Lab Database Exposed 1.3M Records, COVID Test Info. [Website] Retrieved from: https://www.bankinfosecurity.com/lab-database-leak-a-24168

[31] Juneja. P. (n.d.). Limitations & Disadvantages of Decision Support. [Website] https://managementstudyguide.com/limitations-and-disadvantages-of-decision-support-systems.htm

7

Psychology of Industrial Organizational Cybersecurity Leadership

Learning Objectives

- Distinguish industrial organizational psychology.
- Distinguish the role of industrial organizational psychology and cybersecurity leadership.
- Determine the value of organizational training procedures.
- Assess the significance of confidentiality for personnel information and compliance policy.

7.1 Introduction

The consistent changing landscape of cybersecurity has forced organizations and corporations to increase focus on effectively securing information systems, technology, and information assets. Since cybersecurity is consistently changing, industrial organizational (I/O) psychologists have become instrumental in supporting organizations and corporations in preparing their employees to play a role in preventing the organization or corporation from being successfully victimized by cybercriminals. After all, cybercriminals are targeting organizations and corporations because these entities possess employee and customer information, including birthdate, social security number, home address, driver's license numbers, passport information as well as trade secrets, intellectual property, and banking information. Thus, corporations and organizations are partnering with I/O psychologists to increase strategies on how to train and prepare employees to thwart cyberattacks. Partnering with I/O psychologists can help improve employees' cognitive thinking skills. Thus, this chapter explains why I/O psychology is important. This chapter also explains why I/O psychology can benefit organizations and corporations in protecting their information assets and personnel from cyberattack.

I/O psychology uses psychological ideas and theories and applies those theories to the workplace. I/O psychology examines and studies employee behavior and attitude, and employers' interpersonal relationships with their workforce. I/O psychology examines the motivational level of employees as a group before individually. I/O psychology examines individuals and corporate performance in the context of group culture and climate of the organization, and the association shared between people and their job role and responsibilities. Training in the theories of behavior in the workplace require in-depth knowledge of attitudes, career development, decision-making, group therapy, human performance, job analysis, and individual assessment.

For more than 10 years, I/O psychologists have played an important role in the development of mental tests and the usage of these tests in supporting corporations and organizations. A significant component of these tests focuses on personality characteristics, which are increasingly important in helping understand and predict work behavior. Thus, mental tests are used in hiring and retention of employees. Many I/O psychologists are focused on improving productivity and reducing counterproductivity behavior including turnover and absenteeism. However, all I/O psychologists address issues of recruitment, selection, and placement, training and development, performance measurements, workplace motivation, and reward systems. I/O psychologists also look at the quality of work life, structure of daily work, human engagement, corporate development, and consumer behavior. Most populations affected by the influence of I/O psychology, include individuals and applicants to business, industry, labor, and academic. I/O psychologists utilize the following skills and procedures to address human and organizational problems. First, they identify training and development needs and design and optimize work and quality of life. They also create and implement training programs and evaluate the effectiveness of each training program to motivate and coach employees. I/O psychologists also create criteria to evaluate employees and corporate performance and assess customer satisfaction and marketing strategies.

The domain of I/O psychology is sometimes referred to as "work psychology" and expands beyond the physical boundaries of the workplace, due to various variables that can influence work behavior that is not always found in the workplace. These variables include family responsibilities, cultural influence, employment-related legislation, and nonwork events such as cyberattacks. I/O psychology concentrates on the reciprocal impact of work on both life and life as it influences the work environment. I/O psychology combines research and ideas from social psychology and organizational behavior. This discipline addresses the emotional and motivational side of

Table 7.1 Cyber threats.

Type of threats	Reason	Example
Espionage, terrorism, and warfare	• Loss of life • Economic turmoil • Disruption of operations	• Anonymous groups hack corporations.
Inside threat employee	• Maliciousness • Personal or financial gain • Ideological change • Carelessness	• An employee creates a backdoor to help an outside influencer.
Professional hackers	• Maliciousness • Personal or financial gain	• An individual sponsored by a foreign agent exploits weaknesses in an organization's system to steal employees' identifying data.
Amateurs	• Maliciousness • Personal or financial gain	• An individual sends a phishing email to an employee's computer to gain access to login information and customer credit card information.

work, which includes topics, i.e., attitudes, fairness, motivation, stress, leadership, teams, and the broader aspects of organizational and work design. However, I/O psychology shy away from larger issues, including poverty, unemployment, globalization, cyber threats, and work force diversity.

And due to overwhelming growth of malware, information loss, and network threats, the need to examine these threats beyond security and computers should also incorporate I/O psychology to determine factors associated with employee behavior that correlates with the existence of human error and cyberattacks deployed against organizations or corporations. In fact, although technology exists with the development for human input; it is important to also consider the human aspect of engagement with information technology. [1] For example, an individual creates a virus and sends an email to another individual's computer, invoking the receiver to open the email to unleash the virus. It is the engagement shared between two individuals that make the attack possible. Looking at Table 7.1, you can learn about additional cyber threats that can occur due to human engagement.

Thus, one goal of I/O psychology intervention is to focus on improving the entire organization's operation and to address the issues at the core or source, by altering work structure, processes, and systems. This goal is to design a healthier and safer workplace. When I/O psychologists are planning and implementing organizational interventions, they develop theories to implement change. These theories help guide the I/O psychologist to design and execute interventions and help evaluate their effectiveness. This is a strategy that enables corporations and organizations to begin improving how employees respond to cyberattacks.

I/O psychologists are in the position to support and guide organizations and corporations toward developing methods and strategies to fight cyberattacks. I/O psychologists who work with cyber psychologists can become helpful in developing guidelines and framework to help corporations and organizations deter successful cyber threats. This establishes the reason why I/O psychologists are instrumental in helping organizations and corporations deter cyberattacks. [2] Thus, corporations and organizations need to increase partnerships with I/O psychologists to enhance their cybersecurity leadership.

7.2 I/O Psychologists' Obligation to Cybersecurity

I/O psychologists have various roles in corporations and organizations. I/O psychologists are involved in human resources, ethics, company morale, production, and employee relations. One area commonly overlooked by I/O psychologists is their role in data security. The nature of their work internally and externally, requires I/O psychologists to have access to and collect private sensitive information, during the hiring of candidates, especially middle managers and senior leadership from different states and countries. When this information is collected all that information becomes vulnerable to cybersecurity risk, and I/O psychologists are often unaware if an organization or corporation, they work with are deploying effective methods to protect this information.

Modifying the way corporations and organizations and their employees use and interact with the Internet is a priority. When I/O psychology and cybersecurity is paired, it improves behavior and communication that enables corporations and organizations to improve the workplace toward becoming a safer environment. Cybersecurity and I/O psychologists can investigate a wide range of topics from social media, outside forces, or individuals, and raise awareness of cybersecurity risks. After all, some significant components of cybersecurity are securing information, systems, and other valuable commodities from theft or manipulation by electronic means. [3]

Therefore, I/O psychologists utilize job analysis as the building block of all other activities and functions, they perform in the company. I/O psychologists must consider the end user and their behavior, when developing job analysis. Procedures need to be developed to help employees understand the organization's or corporation's email procedures to ensure a safe and secure system. These procedures need to be clearly written and define email security practices. Corporations and organizations need to offer training and resources, conduct simulated phishing exercises, and monitor and review email activity. These procedures also need to enforce email password development techniques and enforce employees change their passwords every 30 days for safety.

Procedures should also explain methods to effectively investigate an email and any email attachments. The end user should investigate any URL that was sent within the email before they click on the link, which may lead to a download page for malware. Procedures should train employees to never give away personal information in an email. Since the COVID-19 crisis, corporations and organizations have experienced tremendous threats targeting employee's email. The persistent change in cybersecurity and remote employees has made it increasingly important for organizations and corporations to pay closer attention to securing information and their corporate or organizational email systems.

The lines between work and leisure time have become blurred and employees use company issued devices and resources for personal use, including social media, online shopping, and telehealth, which increases the potential risks for cyberattacks. Although network firewalls are effective in keeping hackers from accessing corporation's data and email services, some of the apps used by employees for personal email, social media, and video conferencing, also creates more vulnerabilities. Knowing when a cyberattack has taken place can be challenging for any employee to recognize. Thus, I/O psychologists need to educate employees about what to look for. Employees need to be aware that hackers can hijack their webcams on their laptop, which provides hackers access to files, messages, and browser history. Other signs to consider is increased data usage, and battery performance. Employees also need to be aware of hearing clicks or static on the device, and be aware of strange texts messages, email, phone calls, and additional signs to assess if they have been hacked.

Despite employees working outside the company remotely, cybersecurity and I/O psychologist have less direct oversight over employees, and this heightens the chance of unintentional and malicious exposure or loss of corporate data. [4] Thus, I/O psychologists and IT management need to make sure employees understand current policies and procedures while they are working remotely to protect information assets. All policies need to be updated to include and address the heightened security risk associated with remote work. These policies must ensure the organization's security policies, procedures, and protections address new threats that impact remote workplaces.

The European Union's General Data Protection Regulation (GDPR) outlines protection requirements for personal, sensitive data, and companies within the EU and requires companies to document information they have, who can access that information, and where the information is stored. [5] The United States also have federal laws regarding the security of company data and protection requirements. First, the Privacy Act of 1974 governs how federal agencies can collect data and use that data about individuals. The act also prohibits agencies from disclosing an individual's personal information without written consent from that individual. [6] I/O psychologist need to be aware of the Privacy Act of 1974 and how to help corporations or organizations protect their information. President Bill Clinton signed into law the Health Insurance Portability and Accountability Act (HIPAA) in 1996, which created standards for how healthcare providers and insurance companies determine on how they may use patients' health information. HIPAA regulations only apply to certain entities such as doctors, psychologists,' dentists, nurses, healthcare insurance companies, and any company that processes medical information. HIPAA requires all covered entities not use or share any healthcare information without an individual's written consent.

Another important law was signed by President Bill Clinton named the Gramm–Leach–Bliley Act (GLBA) mandated in 1998. This law governs data privacy for financial institutions and companies that offer consumers financial products such as loans, investment advice, and insurance. This law requires financial institutions to have a policy to protect consumer information from security threats such as cyber threats and must provide consumers with a privacy notice explaining what information is collected and how that information is used and shared with whom. This law gives United States consumers the right to opt out of having their information shared with third parties.

Thus, organizations and corporations have an obligation to protect their information assets and intellectual property from cyber threats. This obligation includes training employees about safety measures to use when accessing the Internet and the value of adhering to the training provided to maintain the cybersecurity level established by the organization or corporation. With the increased reliance on computer networks in the workplace, there must be an increased awareness of cyberattack methods, which is commonly overshadowed by an intensity and sophistication deployed by cybercriminals. This invokes the change of role I/O psychologist play in helping corporations and organizations thwart cyberattacks. [7]

Another issue that must be considered and assessed for increased security is intellectual property owned by corporations and organizations, which affects individuals, companies, and countries. While working with corporations and organizations, I/O psychologists will deal with confidentiality involving employees and company information. Therefore, corporations and organizations need to develop cybersecurity protection policy, and that policy must be adhered to. This establishes another reason why I/O psychologists need to work with executive leaders and the human resource department in creating effective policy and outlining penalties for noncompliance. Developing company policy for the protection of employee personal information and intellectual property is very important and must be a high priority for I/O psychologists.

The loss of intellectual property could mean the loss of an item being developed for the marketplace, which can lead to a loss of income generated by the product and a greater loss to the company. Intellectual property loss occurs when employees take documents, disks, or prototypes before they are published by the corporation. Organizations need to conduct reviews of suppliers to ensure they have appropriate security measures in place and comply with regulations. Sharing data between organizations brings many benefits and help reduce costs. This exchange of information comes at a cost and creates risks such as data breaches, theft of intellectual property, and misuse of data. To manage the risk of supplier disruption of cyberattack, suppliers can implement a supplier assessment process. The process includes identifying suppliers, conducting risk assessments, and upgrading supplier security questionnaires. Tables 7.2 and 7.3 provide examples of risk and security assessment questionnaires.

When sensitive information such as financial or customer information is compromised, this can lead to reputation damage, legal damage, and financial losses. [8] If suppliers use intellectual property that was stolen, it can harm the organization's competitive advantage and lead to loss of revenue. Sharing data with suppliers can increase the risk of data misuse, such as data that is not used as intended. Thus, organizations should establish clear guidelines and procedures for sharing data to reduce risk, which includes ownership, security, and confidentiality. To help, the United States government issued the Cybersecurity Information Sharing Act of 2015 (CISA), which authorizes companies to share information, monitor, and implement defense measures on their information system.

Table 7.2 Supplier risk assessment questionnaire.

Supplier risk assessment questionnaire	
Question	**Response**
Are policies and standards based on industry-accepted standards and practices?	Yes or no
Do the information security policies contain statements concerning the organization's definition of information security, objective, and principles to guide all activities relating to information security?	Yes or no
Do owners review and update policies if significant changes occur in legal, business, organizational or technical conditions?	Yes or no
Have all information security policies and standards been reviewed in the last 12 months?	Yes or no
Does the organization's board of directors or ownership require management to regularly demonstrate that the information security program meets its intended objectives?	Yes or no
Are information security personnel responsible for the creation and review of information security policies?	Yes or no
Do the information security personnel maintain professional security certifications?	Yes or no
Does the information security personnel maintain contact with information security special interest groups, specialist security forums or professional associations?	Yes or no
Does the information security personnel participate in continuing education programs?	Yes or no
Is there use of firewall and VPN?	Yes, no, or both
Is there use of encryption to protect sensitive data and messages?	Yes, no, or both

The CISA authorizes companies to monitor and create defensive devises on their own information system to counter any cyber threats and provides certain protection to help companies voluntarily share information about cyber threat indicators and defensive measures with federal, state, local governments, and other companies. [9] These protections include liability, and protection from Freedom of Information Act (FOIA) disclosure. When sharing information about cyberattacks to federal, state, and local governments, companies have a duty to remove any personal information to protect employees and the public. The CISA does not force companies to comply with the act, it is the decision of the company whether to share the cyberattack or keep it confidential. Companies willing to share cybersecurity information with public and private partners should become a part of a comprehensive cybersecurity program defined by the sharing of this information, which

Table 7.3 Supplier security assessment questionnaire.

Supplier security assessment questionnaire	
Question	**Descriptions**
What is the supplier's tier rating?	Tier 1, Tier 2, Tier 3, or Tier 4
What region(s) of the organization are impacted?	North America, Europe, Middle East, Africa, or Asia Pacific
What methods of connectivity does the supplier maintain with the organization?	Electronic data interchange (EDI), application programming interfaces (APIs), cloud-based collaboration tools, secure file transfer protocol (SFTP) or web-based portals
What volume of organization data does the supplier maintain that may have been exposed?	Number of records, year of earliest record, etc.
What type of data does the supplier have access to?	Client data, associate data, board materials, internal budgets, internal policies and procedures, disclosed investment data or public data
If this supplier fails to meet its obligations, do we have a regulatory violation?	Yes or no
Will the supplier provide products or services directly to clients?	Yes or no

broadens the pool of information both government and other companies can use to defend against cyberattacks. This act did not change the cybersecurity landscape. However, it does allow for greater information sharing to create greater defense measures against cyberattacks.

7.3 Understanding Inside Threats

Cyber threats to business have been a priority for cybersecurity personnel to identify, but cyber threats can also come from inside the company. Internal attacks are carried out for financial gain and is becoming increasingly apparent that direct and indirect means are being used to identify human resource vulnerabilities that can be manipulated. [10] Inside threats have become more frequent due to employees feeling underpaid and ignored by management. I/O psychologists need to understand the amount of theft that occurs within the organization and develop plans and procedures to combat this situation. Using psychology to understand the motivation behind the individuals causing the theft is important to help deter this situation.

An insider threat is a cybersecurity risk that is deployed by someone inside the organization, who can be a current or former employee, and who has direct access to the company network, sensitive data, or intellectual property. Such individuals often have knowledge of the company polices and other information that can help them carry out their attack. Unfortunately, it can be difficult to detect an insider attack. Most security tools are focused on preventing and identifying external threats and are not designed to detect inside threats.

There are two types of insider threats: malicious and negligent threats. A malicious insider threat is one that is planned by a disgruntled employee or former employees, who targets the company for financial gain or for vengeance. Some of these incidents can be linked to criminal or illicit cases such as fraud or IP theft. An insider malicious threat can involve selling, sharing, modifying, or deleting confidential information. A negligent insider threat can occur due to human error, carelessness, or manipulation. These threats do not involve individuals acting in bad faith, anyone can be a negligent insider if they share sensitive data, use weak passwords, lose a device, or fall victim to a social engineering attack. The scope of a social engineering attack can lead to a large scale cyberattack, which commonly includes malware or ransomware attacks.

Many organizations are aware of the impact of insider cyber threats; unfortunately, most are more prepared for external cyber threats. Surveys assessed in 2015 report that 3.6% of the total IT budget for the previous year was spent on internal security. [11] Intel Security 2016 report shows that companies experiencing data breaches reveal insiders are more responsible for 43% of data loss, which was considered intentional and malicious. Many organizations feel open to insider threats, and leaders report they are having a hard time detecting and preventing an insider attack but are prepared for external cyberattacks.

These internal breaches can extend far beyond the financial cost, damage the reputation of the company, and affect the personal safety of employees. Most organizations do not have a formal internal threat program, although many organizations have a reactive program. The programs are designed to look at employee behavior such as unauthorized downloads and server logins. Most programs only notify the company after something has gone wrong. In behavioral science research, certain negative emotions, stressors, and conflicts have been associated with workplace aggression, employee turnover, absenteeism, fraud, and sabotage. I/O psychologists can use their training in behavioral science and develop policies and procedures to profile employee negative behaviors.

Furthermore, recent development of software tools can use algorithms to analyze emails and other communication to look for security risks. Today, organizations are using technology and psychological insight to examine employee risk profiles and to uncover concerning changes in behavior, over a long period, by analyzing employees' digital communications. Companies need to have steps in place to detect and prevent insider threats. The most important tool to prevent insider malicious threats is using background checks when hiring a new employee; this will help prevent and mitigate insider security threats by reducing the risks before hiring the employee. [12] Furthermore, multi-factor authentication usage has become essential and more advanced. This is beneficial because it helps prevent weak passwords from being used by careless employees. Therefore, organizations and corporations need to monitor their network traffic by utilizing managed detection and response (MDR) tools to detect cyber threats.

7.4 Summary

Industrial organizational psychologists use human psychological concepts to examine behavior in the workplace, communication, workers investment in the company, job satisfaction, and employee productivity. I/O psychologist examine employee safety, company safety, and the workplace environment, including the culture of a company. Trained I/O psychologists can quickly assess a company; examine barriers and inefficiencies and threats relating to physical and cyber threats. The I/O psychologist can also develop evidence-based procedures for cyber threats and insider threats to help make a company safer. Since cybersecurity has become important to all corporations, industrial organizational psychologists need to be involved in developing a secure culture in the workplace that protects the company and employees from cyberattacks. The I/O psychologist can identify issues and potential problems and use research to choose the best solution for the problem. I/O psychologists can be useful in developing policies, procedures, and environment risk management for the workplace. I/O psychologists can also develop plans for improving organizational structure. Due to the extensive training in human behavior and managing workplace issues, I/O psychologists can help identify issues – i.e., cyberattacks and insider cyber threats, and help improve how corporations and organizations protect themselves from losses. I/O psychologists can conduct research that enable them to improve how they help businesses achieve their goals. They can also help develop personality assessments to help corporations and organizations select trustworthy employees. I/O psychologist can conduct observational research that helps them monitor several different organizations or corporations determine which management strategies work best and how. An I/O psychologist can also do research relating to operations within a company and use that data to analyze, organize, and create clarity of information to improve decision-making that helps with problem-solving.

Cyber threats and counteracting intellectual property loss have become a major issue with all corporations and organizations. Therefore, protecting information assets and systems from hackers is a full-time management responsibility. I/O psychologists need to understand the importance of fighting against hackers and the impact of losing control over intellectual property. An I/O psychologist is now instrumental in dealing with employees' daily business operations, communication, and engagement as it relates to the management of corporate or organizations' information assets and information systems. Thus, increasing the involvement of I/O psychology in helping corporations or organizations develop plans and polices to protect against unauthorized intrusion is essential.

7.5 Discussion Questions

1. What can I/O psychologist help improve with employees?
2. What do I/O psychologist examine as a group before individually?
3. What do I/O psychologist utilize as the building block of all other activities and functions, they perform?
4. What do employees use for personal email, social media, and video conferencing that creates more vulnerabilities for a corporation or organization?
5. Who needs to make sure employees understand current policies and procedures while working remotely to protect information assets?
6. What does the European Union's General Data Protection Regulation outline?
7. What Act governs how federal agencies can collect data and use that data about individuals?
8. Who do HIPAA regulations apply to?

9. What does the Cybersecurity Information Sharing Act of 2015 (CISA) authorizes?
10. What can I/O psychologist use to profile employee negative behaviors?

Glossary

Embedded processors – embedded processors are a computer system, a combination of computer processors, computer memory, and input/output peripheral devises that have a dedicated function.

Intellectual property – refers to the creations, such as inventions, literary, artistic works, designs, symbols, names, and images used in commerce.

Maliciousness – intending to harm someone, or something, or the transmission of harmful software such as computer viruses.

Managed detection and response (MDR) – is a cybersecurity service that helps proactively protect organizations from cyber threats using advanced detection and rapid incident response.

Negligent insider – is an employee that does not follow proper IT procedures, this can include not logging off, downloading software online without permission, allowing others into the company computer system.

References

[1] Dreibelbis, R. C., Martin, J., Coovert, M. D., & Dorsey, D. W. (2018). The Looming Cybersecurity Crisis and What It Means for the Practice of Industrial and Organizational Psychology. Industrial and Organizational Psychology, 11(2), 346–365. doi:10.1017/iop.2018.3

[2] Peter Trim, & David Upton. (2013). Cyber Security Culture: Counteracting Cyber Threats Through Organizational Learning and Training. Routledge.

[3] Dreibelbis, R. C., Martin, J., Coovert, M. D., & Dorsey, D. W. (2018). The Looming Cybersecurity Crisis and What It Means for the Practice of Industrial and Organizational Psychology. Industrial and Organizational Psychology, 11(2), 346–365. doi:10.1017/iop.2018.3

[4] Pratt, M. K. (2022, August). Remote Work Cybersecurity: 12 Risks and How to Prevent Them. Search Security. https://www.techtarget.com/searchsecurity/tip/Remote-work-cybersecurity-12-risks-and-how-to-prevent-them

[5] Peter Trim, & David Upton. (2013). Cyber Security Culture: Counteracting Cyber Threats Through Organizational Learning and Training. Routledge.

[6] Murray, C. (n.d.). U.S. Data Privacy Protection Laws: A Comprehensive Guide. Forbes. Retrieved March 29, 2024, from https://www.forbes.com/sites/conormurray/2023/04/21/us-data-privacy-protection-laws-a-comprehensive-guide/?sh=49a0658f5f92

[7] Trim, P. R. J., & Lee, Y.-I. (2019). The role of B2B marketers in increasing cyber security awareness and influencing behavioral change. Industrial Marketing Management, 83, 224–238. https://doi-org.ezproxy.snhu.edu/10.1016/j.indmarman.2019.04.003

[8] Green, C. (2023). Best practices in supplier relationship management and response when supply is disrupted by cyber-attack: An incident response framework. Journal of Business Continuity & Emergency Planning, 17(1), 6–15.

[9] Karp, B. (2015). Federal Guidance on the Cybersecurity Information Sharing Act of 2015. Harvard.edu. https://corpgov.law.harvard.edu/2016/03/03/federal-guidance-on-the-cybersecurity-information-sharing-act-of-2015/

[10] Peter Trim, & David Upton. (2013). Cyber Security Culture: Counteracting Cyber Threats Through Organizational Learning and Training. Routledge.

[11] Stroz, E., Weber, S., & Shaw, E. (2016, September 20). Psychology Is the Key to Detecting Internal Cyberthreats. Harvard Business Review. https://hbr.org/2016/09/psychology-is-the-key-to-detecting-internal-cyberthreats

[12] Van Zeveloff, M. (2016, September 19). The Biggest Cybersecurity Threats Are Inside Your Company. Harvard Business Review. https://hbr.org/2016/09/the-biggest-cybersecurity-threats-are-inside-your-company

Index

About the Authors

Bradley Fowler, PhD earned a Collaborative Institute Training Initiative (CITI) Certificate in Doctoral Research at Capitol Technology University in September 2022 before earning a Master of Research in Cyberpsychology from Capitol Technology University in 2023-Summa Cum Laude. Mr. Fowler also earned a Master of Science in Cybersecurity in 2018-Summa Cum Laude and a Master of Science in Managing Information Systems in 2021-Summa Cum Laude both from Bellevue University; a Master of Science in Cloud Computing Architecture in 2022-Cum Laude and a Graduate Certificate in Information Assurance in 2023 both from University of Maryland Global Campus. Furthermore, he earned a Master of Public Policy in Cybersecurity Policy from American Public University Systems in 2022-Summa Cum Laude, and he earned a Bachelor of Arts in eMarketing in 2015-Cum Laude, a Master of Arts in Teaching and Learning with Technology in 2016-Summa Cum Laude, and Master of Science in Technology Management in 2024-Magna Cum Laude, all from University of Arizona Global Campus. And in December 2023, he completed a Graduate certificate in Human Resource Management from Wilmington University.

Currently, Mr. Fowler is completing a Doctor of Management Information Systems and Technology at University of Phoenix and conducting research for a Doctor of Education in Education Administration dissertation at California Coast University. He is also completing his dissertation defense for his PhD in Cybersecurity Leadership at Capitol Technology University, with a 2024 conferral date. He is a general alumni member at University of Maryland Global Campus, member of the E-Learning Guild, member of the Webmaster Association, member of the National Cybersecurity Student Association; a peer review analyst for the National Cyberwatch Association, lifetime member of the Golden Key International Honour Society, and lifetime member of the National Society of Leadership and Success (NSLS), which he is currently the Editor of the University of Phoenix NSLS chapter Newsletter. Additionally, Mr. Fowler is Master Chair and Adjunct Professor with Capitol Technology University, and co-author of *Cybersecurity Public Policy SWOT Analysis for 43 Countries*, author of *AWS for Public and*

Private Sector Cloud Computing Architecture for Government and Business, and author of *Information Assurance Risk Management Strategies for Managing Information Systems and Technology in the Cloud*, and co-author of *Cyberpsychology Can Help Us Understand Cybercrime.*

*Contact Mr. Fowler for speaking engagements, interviews, or conference invites, by emailing him at drbfowler@mailfence.com

Bruce G. Chaundy earned a Bachelor of Arts in Psychology from University of Arizona Global Campus before pursuing a Master of Science in Psychology at American Public University System, and before completing a Master of Science in Industrial Organizational Psychology at Southern New Hampshire University. Mr. Chaundy managed Detroit Electrical Coatings, LLC., as the Purchasing Manager before becoming the Purchasing Manager for Axxis Corporation. He has more than 40 years' experience working with corporate personnel. Mr. Chaundy is a lifetime member of the Phi Theta Kappa International Honor Society.

For Product Safety Concerns and Information please contact our EU
representative GPSR@taylorandfrancis.com
Taylor & Francis Verlag GmbH, Kaufingerstraße 24, 80331 München, Germany

www.ingramcontent.com/pod-product-compliance
Lightning Source LLC
Chambersburg PA
CBHW070250260926
51849CB00001BA/94
9788770042345